KEVIN MOORE'S

HAIL MARY PASS

INTO THE END ZONE WITH THE 49ERS IN LEVI'S STADIUM

Photo by: John P. Dixon

Moore & Moore

P.O. Box 286, Santa Clara, CA 95052

Moore & Moore publications are available at special discounts for bulk purchases for sales promotions, premiums, fund raising, or educational use.

For details contact: Moore & Moore

HailMaryPassBook.com

Kevin Moore's HAIL MARY PASS

INTO THE END ZONE WITH THE

49ERS IN LEVI'S STADIUM

ISBN – 978-0-578-15086-4

Book Design & Layout by Mark Gardner / Iguana Design & Print

and Kevin Moore, Michael Fallon, W.J. Parolini

Manufactured in Santa Clara CA USA

Cover front + back by Tao Productions LLC / Tao 3D Solutions

And Mark Gardner / Iguana Design and Print

Kevin Moore cover photo by Raymond R. Rodriquez, Jr.

The Catch photo by Frederic Larson / San Francisco Chronicle / Polaris

First Edition, August 2015

10 9 8 7 6 5 4 3 2 1

TABLE OF EPISODES

FOREWORD

By Dwight Clark, Brent Jones, John Faylor

As most football fans know, a "Hail Mary Pass" is a very long forward pass made in desperation with only a small chance of success. Prior to the Hail Mary Pass, a desperation pass was notably called the "Alley-Oop," employed in the 1950s by our own San Francisco 49er greats, quarterback Y.A. Tittle and receiver R.C. Owens. Then on January 10, 1982, with the help of the genius coach Bill Walsh, quarterback Joe Montana, myself as wide-receiver, and the rest of the 49ers, we carried on that tradition of last minute heroics with a play known in the 49ers playbook as "Red Right Tight – Sprint Right Option"–now more famously called "The Catch."

I am honored that Kevin chose this classic description and photo of The Catch for the cover of his book, and invited me, and my former 49er teammates Brent Jones and John Faylor, to write the Foreword for Kevin Moore's Hail Mary Pass ~ Into the End Zone with the 49ers in Levi's Stadium.

In 2004, the San Francisco 49ers organization was running out of suitable locations to build a new state-of-the-art NFL stadium in San Francisco city proper. Our current home at Candlestick Park was deteriorating quickly, and a new NFL stadium had not been built in California since the early 1960s. It was certainly time for a Hail Mary…and so entered Kevin Moore, Forty-Niner Faithful and more fortuitous, future Santa Clara Vice-Mayor.

Kevin, through his hard work and never-say-die attitude, became a major driving force in bringing the San Francisco 49ers to the negotiating table with the City of Santa Clara. In June of 2010, the voters of Santa Clara passed the Santa Clara 49ers Stadium Measure, opening the way for a new home for the 49ers and their Faithful. Four years later, LEVI'S Stadium was inaugurated! And to boot, the prestigious Super Bowl 50 in February 2016 will be hosted there–at LEVI'S Stadium.

This book will take you on an entertaining and informative journey through behind-the-scene stories seldom shared in public. You will be surprised at the history and circumstances that culminated in LEVI's Stadium. You will have a look into and through the eyes, yea, the heart and soul, of Kevin Moore.

–Dwight Clark, San Francisco 49ers

When writing a book about a political process, subtle aspects that were critical elements may be easily overlooked, and/or the banalities may be sugar-coated. This is not the case in Kevin Moore's book. As a proud Santa Clara University graduate like Kevin, I am delighted to see the backdrop that our Alma Mater affords this story. Emanating from games played at Buck Shaw Stadium, named after the first 49ers head coach, Buck Shaw, stories were made and told and little did we know folded into a story leading up to the San Francisco 49ers making a home in Santa Clara. Kevin goes the distance in telling the real stories, from sneaking into our 49ers locker room and celebrating alongside team members, to sitting down with VIPs in closed-door meetings at team headquarters. Kevin has always been a 49ers Faithful, and now we can appreciate his role in bringing the 49ers to Santa Clara.

-- *Brent Jones, San Francisco 49ers*

As a long-time friend of Kevin Moore, I am excited to be part of the team writing the foreword for Kevin's book. This honor is even more special because I join two other long-time friends and 49er teammates, legendary All-Pro 49ers Dwight Clark and Brent Jones; Brent and I are also proud Santa Clara University Broncos.

I had the pleasure and delight of growing up with Kevin in Santa Clara. We attended grammar school together at St. Justin where Kev avoided the wrath of nuns, and classmates voted him "friendliest person." We enjoyed memborable times at Archbishop Mitty High School, and shared dreams at the classic SCU neighboring waterholes, The Hut and Lord John's. This loveable fellow has not changed in 40 years! Kev is always wishing persons love, and Kevin is loved in return. He is a quality human being, one who works constantly to make our community a better place for everyone.

Kev and I play poker virtually every week with a group of friends. Some weeks I win, some weeks he wins; the game is always filled with hours of laughter and true fellowship. In the game of life you always want Kevin on your side; you will never find a more loyal friend. When Kev is working on a project or leading an effort, he is a heat-seeking missile. You want him on your team and in your corner, and no matter how desperate the situation, never bet against him getting things done.

From the time Kevin began talking about bringing the San Francisco 49ers to our little city of Santa Clara, while many others laughed, I believed he could do it. They are not laughing now. Kevin's Hail Mary Pass was caught for a touchdown, and our Mission City scored the 49ers!

-- *John Faylor, San Francisco 49ers*

PREFACE

People believed in him. They wanted to believe in the Dream, and he was proof that it WAS. His name was Francis, and he lived and died quietly and peacefully in Assisi (Italy)...He left behind a Dream to dream and a Journey to challenge every man.

Both are important,
The Journey and the Dream,
Both are important,
The coming-out and the entering-in.
Without the Journey
The Dream is a futile entering into yourself
Where you ride a monotonous wheel
That spins around you alone.
With the Journey
The entering-in is itself a Journey
That does not end inside you
But passes through the self and
Out the other side of you
Where you ride the wheel
You found inside.
The Journey and the Dream
Are one balanced act of love
And both are realized
Outside the mind.

-- Murray Bodo, O.F.M.,
from his book on St. Francis of Assisi

Kevin Moore is no St. Francis, he'd be first to admit. But he had a Dream and other people who perceived his vision believed in him. Together they realized a dream.

COIN TOSS

Good afternoon, gentlemen, team captains. Our commemorative coin today has the Golden Gate Bridge as heads and Mission Santa Clara as tails. Santa Clara, you're the visiting team, so captain, call it in the air. Santa Clara calls "Tails"…

Good friend Anthony Moore

SANTA CLARA, CALIFORNIA
GO NINERS!

Whether you are a 49er Faithful sitting in the stands of the new Levi's Stadium, a VIP enjoying the amenities of a luxury suite, or a nay sayer in your yard wishing the whole thing was just someone else's pipe dream; there's a compelling story to be told of the circumstances that converged to bring the San Francisco 49ers to Santa Clara, California.

This book is a story of one man's journey to establish a professional sports team in his hometown Santa Clara. He tried first with the San Francisco Giants and then with the Oakland Athletics, but he didn't score until he threw a "Hail Mary Pass" to the San Francisco 49ers.

By all rights, Santa Clara had little chance to attract an NFL team. This small community seemed ill-equipped to host a professional sports franchise and unlikely to wield the financial muscle needed to build a billion dollar stadium. But the dream Kevin Moore pursued was potent enough to attract key players, strong enough to unite a community, and bold enough to land Santa Clara in the end zone with the 49ers.

The author hopes you will forgive him the use of any expletives for which he has confessed and performed penance, the usual "Three Our Fathers and Three Hail Marys."

BMW AND THE BURNING BUSH

On November 8, 2006, I get the phone call. I am invited to the San Francisco 49ers headquarters in Santa Clara. Niners' ownership will make a public statement the following day regarding their interest in a future home for the team. As Santa Clara Vice Mayor and leading liaison to the Niners, I am to be advised of their action by the team executive. My efforts of a lifetime, encouraged by the support of family, friends, and several City colleagues, yet chided by others, could come down to a coin toss.

As luck would have it, my '68 Firebird was being restored, so I jump into my wife's BMW 325i, attach my jumble of real-estate keys to her chain ring and start the engine. I hurry through city streets to the Niners' offices on the site of their Training Facility adjacent to California's Great America. I'm pumped, it feels like "4th and inches" with the game on the line. Something is about to break. I park in the near-empty lot. A security guard heading out shouts "Hey Coach." He assumed I was on the coaching staff because I was so often on site. I ascend the stairs and make my way to the office of Larry MacNeil, Chief Financial Officer. Larry welcomes me.

He says there is going to be an announcement tomorrow. But he cannot tell me exactly what ownership will say. He wanted me to be, the first to know that a decision was coming down. Then his kicker: he was leaving town, going down to Mexico for Baja Racing. I immediately think to myself, "Is MacNeil telling me the whole story? *And* he's leaving town tomorrow–what's that all about? Is the announcement going to light a fuse while he slips quietly away and leaves us here amidst the fireworks?" Despite the uncertainty, I want to believe that the decision will work in our favor. Then again, maybe the cynics at City Hall are right–I must be smoking the crack pipe thinking the Niners could actually land in Santa Clara.

I exit the building feeling optimistic, pumping my fist in the air, then just as quickly doubt sets in. I'm puzzled by the whole scenario. Even if ownership announces that Santa Clara is their number one choice, management could reverse the decision. Maybe they're playing us against San Francisco and in the end the team remains in the City by the Bay. No, I do sense we're in this, I believe we're in the game.

I jump into the BMW, insert the ignition key with the long jumble of keys hanging from it, fire up the engine and reverse out of the parking stall. Anxious and excited as I am, I shift into drive and start to turn but over accelerate the ultimate driving machine sending the car into a spin. The dangling key chain whips around the steering column jamming the wheel. I jerk the wheel back but overcorrect and the car advances across the parking lot and flies into the bushes.

I'm horrified. My BMW is stalled in the bushes in front of the 49ers corporate office. Late working staff are exiting the building. Security cameras are all around. If Niners executives witnessed this calamity they'd surely be asking themselves who is this idiot? In the bush, I'm burning with frustration. If the team is serious about relocating to Santa Clara, did I burn my bridge to the Niners? Did I dash the dream I've held since five years old? Is God telling me this journey is fraught with hazards—proceed with care?

An angel of the Lord appeared to him in a flame of fire out of the midst of a bush; and he looked, and lo, the bush was burning, yet it was not consumed… Exodus 3:2

Buck Shaw Stadium
THE UNIVERSITY OF
SANTA CLARA
BRONCOS
1st
Quarter

KICK-OFF

Such began in earnest and embarrassment a new phase, actually the third phase of a lifelong journey to bring a professional sports team to my little hometown, the Mission City, Santa Clara. I often wondered if one's life purpose is driven by one's childhood dream, or does one walk a path dictated by circumstance or convenience? I have directed my life journey toward this one dream, this one goal. Or, maybe like in *The Hound of Heaven,* this dream has chased me down.

I should disclose at the kick-off of my story that I was diagnosed with ADD - Attention Deficit Disorder. I often ask myself what effect these symptoms have had on my decision-making, my communication style, my daily actions. I have sometimes joked that my "ADD Advantage" has provoked dealing with reality in extraordinary ways that resulted in extraordinary outcomes– for better or for worse! I guess I'm channeling Thoreau's *Walden,* "If one advances confidently in the direction of his dreams, and endeavors to live the life which he has imagined, he will meet with a success unexpected in common hours." But is this true for me, a person who's often a rebel, an antithesis to the status quo, the anti-hero to business as usual? As I attempt to make sense of this, as I reflect back from this burning bush moment; I see, like beads on a rosary, a string of life episodes that were critical plays leading into the end zone with the San Francisco 49ers.

FROM THE MOORE FAMILY SPORTS ARCHIVES

My love of sports was instilled at an early age through my family. My mom and dad both played sports. My mom played softball and rowed crew. My dad played baseball and ran track. Brother Johnny played baseball, sister Reenie played softball and cheered, Annie volleyball and tennis, Emmy played golf, Patty too played various sports. Sports were woven into our family culture. As the youngest sibiling, I was destined to inherit this love of sports.

Dad, brother Johnny and me

I grew up in a Catholic family of six. Mom and dad were good practicing Catholics. Because my brother is 12 years older than me, and my four sisters 11, 10, 9, and 8 years older respectively, I was often spoiled being the youngest. My sisters treated me like one of their treasured dolls. They attended an all girls' school and would sometimes bring me with them. They, along with their friends, showered me with attention. Our family was filled with love.

When things aren't going well, it's a consolation and a blessing to reflect on the love that my parents and siblings instilled.

While other families on the block had Dough-boy pools in their backyards, we had a pitching mound! My brother was an all-star pitcher. Our father always had time after work to play a game of catch with us. We had regular ballgames on our street. Of course I collected and traded baseball cards and posted pictures of sports heroes on my bedroom walls.

I attended St. Justin Catholic School on Homestead Avenue in Santa Clara. We were a sports powerhouse. Our coach George Santich was the perfect role model for a bunch of rambunctious kids. He taught us how to play with style and grace. Considering my religious leanings, oddly enough I was never an altar boy who served at Mass.

With Coach George Santich

FIVE-YEAR-OLD KID STORY: SF GIANTS VS SC BRONCOS

I remember in particular one morning of my childhood. I was in the living room on the hassock in front of the TV, watching Speed Racer and eating Cheerios. My beloved baseball glove was next to me and I was feeling excited about plans for the day. My sisters were streaming through the house, dressed in their plaid skirts, common attire for parochial schools at the time. I remember mom reminding my older sister, Annie, that today was the day that she was to take me to the baseball game at Santa Clara University. Every spring Santa Clara University played an exhibition against the San Francisco Giants.

I was in kindergarten at Westwood School in a class for late readers when Annie and her friend Noney showed up with a note for the teacher. While the other kids sat there watching I grabbed my glove and left. My sister drove us to the SCU campus and parked in front of the Mission Church. We three walked with haste to the stadium for the Broncos vs. Giants game. Now mind you, this is the first time I've been taken out of school for something other than a doctor's appointment. I couldn't believe my luck; I was headed to see the San Francisco Giants play baseball!

I distinctly remember the magical feeling of entering Buck Shaw Stadium: the smell of hot dogs, the Giants warming up on the field, kids hanging over fences for autographs. "Wow, this is the greatest! It's like a carnival, a circus. It's amazing."

It was the fourth inning and I was loving it. It was a beautiful Northern California afternoon, the sun was high and bright. The scent of peanuts and popcorn filled the air. The crack of the bat coupled with the ensuing crackle of the crowd filled me with excitement. My senses took in every detail of the ballpark and sporting contest. And then all of a sudden my sister announced, "We've got to leave."

"But it's only the fourth inning, they're playing seven innings today. Why can't we stay to the end? Mom said I could stay to the end."

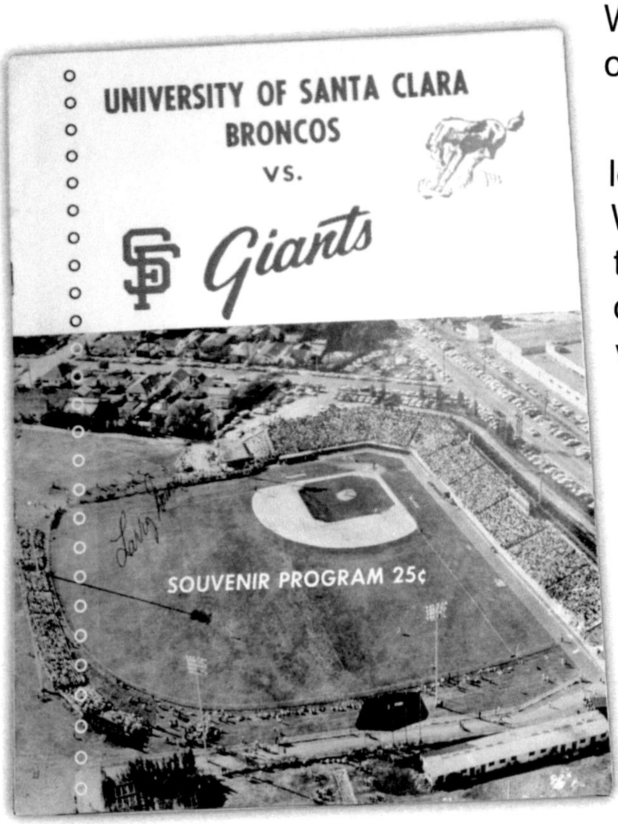

But Annie said, "No, we've got to leave now." We three started walking out. With my head hanging down step-by-step through packed bleachers, I was in utter disbelief. No, no, this was all wrong. We were heading towards the exit gate.

Suddenly an invisible hand reached down and stopped me dead in my tracks. I knew that *this* is where I belonged, right here right now, in this ballpark. As I slowed a few paces trailing behind Annie and Noney, my rebel brain shouted "I can't go." To the right of me I saw an aisle leading up the bleachers; and above it the press box. I made my move, took off, scurried up the steps through all these people and didn't look back. Now high up in the bleachers, I was looking where to hide. Two old guys, older-than-the-hills, sat there with beers in hand and one called out, "Hey, son, where you goin' so fast?"

"Ditching my sister, she wanted to leave early."

"Well who can blame ya, son?" the other agreed. "Come sit with us, we'll hide you from that terrible sister of yours."

It was a different age then, I wasn't to become a Lindbergh baby; so I sat with these two fellows and watched the game through its conclusion. We had a great time!

When the game was over I hung around savoring the sights and sounds of professional baseball, then realized I better hightail it home. I got my bearings–three miles west–and set off through campus. As a five-year-old walking past the 11 floors of Swig Residence Hall, I remember looking up and thinking "that's the tallest building I've ever seen in my life!" When I reached the edge of campus where city streets pointed in every direction and I shuddered. I hadn't a clue how to get home.

Eventually, I found my my way home. My guardian angel must have been working overtime that day. Approaching the front door I saw my mom on watch behind the screen. She exhaled her worry, wiped away a watery tear, and grabbed her missing child. "Why did you leave your sister?"

"You said I could stay 'till the end of the game, but she wanted to leave."

"I guess you're a true baseball fan just like your father," she said hugging me.

Seven years later at the ripe age of twelve I attended another such exhibition. I had broken my arm and was wearing a cast but still had my glove and baseball with me. Outside Buck Shaw Stadium I ran into Bob Lurie, owner of the San Francisco Giants, and my hero for having saved the team from moving away. I called out his name and he turned to me and smiled. I reached out, a baseball in hand and asked, "Mr. Lurie, would you sign my baseball?" Graciously, he did. This signed baseball was one of my early sports treasures and would become like a talisman shining light far into my political future.

Willie Mays playing SCU at Buck Shaw

Courtesy of Santa Clara University Athletics

BETTING ON THE NINERS WITHOUT THE NUNS KNOWING

My parents enrolled me in St. Justin Catholic School. By the second grade I was keeping an eye on the San Francisco 49ers football team as well as the Giants. My first money bet was on the Niners. My buddy Dominik came up to me and said, "This guy in the upper grade is looking to bet anyone on Sunday's football game against the Rams." So I bet a quarter on my team and won a quarter, a thrilling win for a seven-year-old. Then to collect my winnings we snuck down a long school hallway careful to avoid the nuns on our way to the older kids' playground. My buddy Dominik showed no fear as he asked the biggest kid on the playground to pay up.... "Ah, you were just lucky, kid."

My love for both the Giants and Niners grew. My other buddy Scott and I always talked about when we were older moving to Hunters Point near Candlestick Park so we could catch every home game. We never did move there, but my connection to the Giants and later bond with the 49ers was established nonetheless. These became my *home* teams, and in my professional life, pursuit of these teams became an obsession.

IN THE LOCKER ROOM WITH THE NINERS

Some thirteen years after my first quarter bet on the Niners, I came home from college on Christmas break and immediately found myself in my element. My buddy Tom and I were lucky to score tickets to a Dallas Cowboys versus San Francisco 49ers game at Candlestick Park. The Cowboys versus Niners remained a strong rivalry resonating with The Catch of 1982; the year the 49ers broke through the Cowboy stranglehold to win the NFC Championship. The 49ers were in a *must win* game to make the playoffs. The Stick was rocking right through to the end of the game. After a dramatic win, we stormed the field. These were indeed the Walsh and West Coast Offense glory years.

Earlier in my youth, my dad of all people, had given me secrets for gaining entrance to off-limit places. For a stretch of time he and his friend's fail-safe plan was to bring to the locker room several laundered jerseys that his friend's father had purposefully held back from delivering. I had no connections to the team's laundry business, but what I essentially learned from these maneuvers was to have purpose, have confidence, act like I belonged. So after the game I applied the art of gate-crashing. The security guard outside the locker room door was young like me, and he likely suspected that I was attempting to crash the locker room. But I was able to convince him by employing a "Jedi mind trick" (*Star Wars* being big at that time) that I needed to be in the locker room for the post game celebration. He looked me over and said, "I've turned away dozens attempting to enter with every excuse in the book, but for some crazy reason I believe *you* need to be in there with the team."

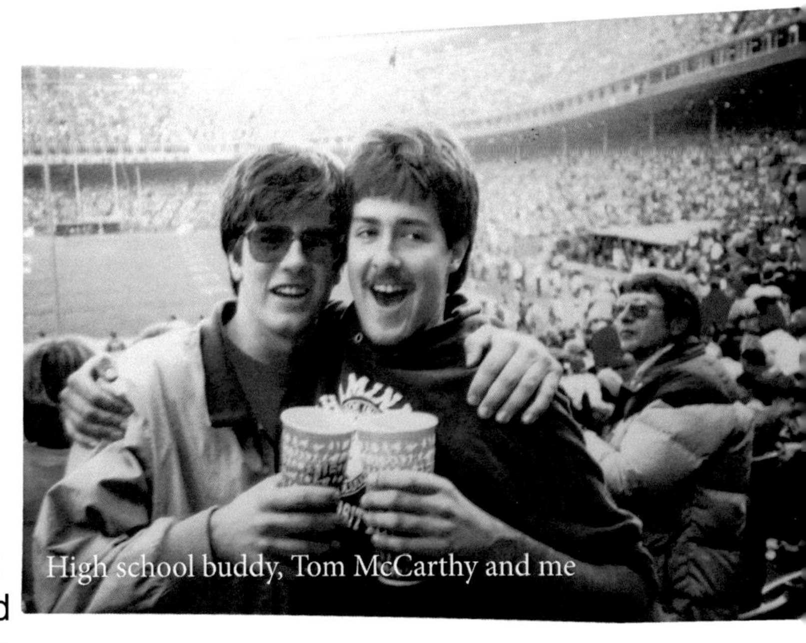
High school buddy, Tom McCarthy and me

"But I don't want you to get in trouble."

"Screw it," he dismissed. "This is the last home game and my last day on the job. Go on in."

I walked down a long hallway. I felt I was walking down a tunnel of light into heaven itself. I approached two massive red doors with large gold handles. The approach was silent and I feared somehow I had headed the wrong direction. I slowly pulled open the massive door and sounds of jubilation flooded out. I was indeed inside the locker room of the Niners! Players I knew by name and admired stood all around. I couldn't believe I was there. I started walking among them, high-fiving members of their famous secondary "Dwight Hicks and the Hot Licks." Then I just stood there in awe of these amazing players and coaches. I was again that innocent five-year-old kid lost in a dream–and that posture gave me away. It unfortunately caught the attention of the senior security officer inside. He asked whose guest was I. Boldly I declared "Ronnie Lott" but he knew I'd made that up–the jig was up.

He graciously said, "you've somehow made it past security, but I'm afraid, young man, I must escort you out." And he did just that–respectfully escorted me toward the door as if I were a VIP and not the gate-crasher I was.

Photo by Michael Fallon

En route to the exit, the interview room door suddenly swung open and out came legendary Coach Bill Walsh himself. In my amazement at this last stroke of good fortune, I stretched out my hand to Coach Walsh; he reciprocated and shook my hand. Before the door slammed shut, from inside the room I got a *head-nod* from both Joe Montana and Dwight Clark that I'll never forget. The gods were surely with me and one could surmise that today was the first time that I was *in the end zone with the San Francisco 49ers!*

HONOLULU PLASTIC DOG PARTY

I spent a good part of the '80s at Chaminade University in Honolulu, Hawaii. The Silverswords basketball team had shockingly upset Ralph Sampson and his No.1 ranked Virginia Cavaliers in 1982. When I arrived at school my goals were simple. The first goal was to stay single, but date a lot of women. That lasted less than a month. I fell in love with a beautiful, fun and extremely intelligent brunette from New Jersey and we dated all four years. My second goal was to be elected Student Body President, an ambitious goal I did accomplish. My third goal was to make the Chaminade Basketball team (bench), which unrealistic achievement was realized. Oh, yes, there was a fourth goal too easily overlooked–graduate with a degree in political science.

I spent all four years living in the Hale Pohaku Dorm, Room #108. The suite had two bedrooms, a living room with a lanai and a view of Diamond Head, a kitchen, a large bathroom and a reputation for throwing legendary parties. Homecoming Week arrived and yours truly was put in charge of the week-long festivities. I decided right off that one of the events, a party, be held in our dorm room and open to the entire student body. The plan sounded rational at the time. But what type party? Toga Party? Nah, we had already perfected that eight times in four years. Septoberfest? Nah, been there, done that. Then it came to me–it's time for a "Plastic Dog Party." With the theme set, we commissioned my roommate, a.k.a. "Guy-Bone," to design a big plastic dog out of large black hefty bags–and man's best friend came out groomed for show. We covered the windows with our mattresses and bed sheets to muffle the loud noise of music blaring at the highest volume. My roommate Tom, a.k.a. "Tom-ass," packed our large bathtub with ice and filled it with beer. Folks partied throughout the night, the party was an absolute rage. By morning the room resembled the opening scene of *The Hangover*. The Plastic Dog was not looking so good, eviscerated on the living room floor.

(Tom Magee and Guy Smith holding a keg)

HONOLULU ADVERTISER NEWSPAPER

"No question, the cleverest adieu to the old drinking law was at Chaminade University. Following a candlelight procession across campus, The Grim Reaper appeared at a midnight funeral for the old law. Students dug a grave for an empty beer keg…"

Late in the morning I was awakened by my slightly sober roommate Randy's loud voice, "Kev, your mom sent you a care package" which he threw down on the bed.

Still drowsy I responded, "Huh, what, a care package? Well could you open it?"

There inside was a Bay Area newspaper. Its headline caught his eye. "Hey, check this out. The Giants are looking to come to Santa Clara."

"Give me that thing." I couldn't believe it but there was a headline in black and white: "Giants Eyeing Santa Clara." I could see into the future: a baseball stadium in my hometown, a place to hang out like when I was young, but now we're talking the big leagues. Could my beloved Giants really come to Santa Clara? Is it possible? Hmmm, this is something I want to be involved with.

Kevin Moore and Kim Camara
"Fun Body Award Winners!"

THE SILVERSWORD NEWSPAPER

"Kevin Moore walked away with the top prize at Bobby Magee's Waikiki, in the "Fun Body Contest" when he got wild and crazy on the dance floor, sacrificing his body by rolling and flipping around on the floor, bringing the crowd to their feet..."

After recovering from homecoming week I visited my favorite place on campus. Chaminade had a beautiful glass chapel looking out over Diamond Head and the Pacific Ocean. I loved to be in that chapel and would go there often and pray. I needed prayer and forgiveness for my many indiscretions. I prayed for a dream to someday come true, a dream and a journey that arose in the islands of Hawaii.

MEANWHILE ... A TRAINING FACILITY FOR THE NINERS

Now while I was away at Chaminade studying, playing sports, managing student government, and yes, drinking beers and dancing on the beaches of Hawaii, in 1986 on the other side of the ocean and unbeknown to me, a development was taking shape in Santa Clara. The outcome of which would be of great significance later in my life and in that of the 49ers. Getting wind of the fact that the San Francisco 49ers were seeking a site for a new Training Facility, the current Mayor, Everett "Eddie" Souza, and City Manager, Don Von Raesfeld, got in touch with Eddie DeBartolo whose family owned the Niners. Eddie and Eddie hit it off. They discovered their families were both from Youngstown, Ohio, not far from Canton and the National Football League Hall of Fame. Mayor Eddie Souza eagerly informed Eddie DeBartolo that Santa Clara owned an 11-acre site near California's Great America. Eddie made Eddie "an offer he couldn't refuse."

A 2006 San Jose Mercury News headline read:

How City Lured Niners

1980s Land Gamble Gave Santa Clara Advantage over SF.

A 2009 San Jose Mercury News article by Mike Swift on the 49ers'

SWEET DEAL

"Two decades ago 49ers owners and coach Bill Walsh stood next to a 9-year old kid named Jed York, now the team president, and cut the ribbon on the Marie P. DeBartolo Sports Center…." Until now, the team headquarters has been a quiet footnote in Santa Clara's intense public debate over whether it should provide $114 million to help build a stadium next door. But the 49ers training facility could be thrust into the fray…. The team wants its headquarters close to its new stadium….Now that we are working on the prospect of having a stadium across the street, we see all sorts of advantages to the players, coaches, staff and for overall operation" (Jed) York said. "If for some reason we are not able to move forward with our plan in Santa Clara, then there is no guarantee that the training facility will remain at this location….“ Not counting players, the headquarters is home to 157 workers, including 21 coaches…. The facility is an anchor for the lives of players and coaches.

THE "SANTA CLARA" GIANTS CAMPAIGN

Back home, in an attempt to gain momentum in a packed public hearing at Santa Clara City Hall where the opposition held sway, I mustered the courage to step forward and speak. Everybody was lining up before the podium including a council candidate who kindly offered that I speak prior to him. I said, "You better be sure because you don't want to speak after me. I've prepared a speech I've been waiting to give my whole life. You won't want to follow that."

I went before the audience and spoke about how good the Giants would be for Santa Clara, then came my piece-de-resistance: "I met Mr. Lurie when I was 12 years old, right outside Buck Shaw Stadium. He signed this baseball for me. He would be equally as gracious to Santa Clara." And I pulled this baseball out of a brown paper bag and held up the ball for all to see. The crowd erupted. When I looked across the Chambers at Mr. Lurie, he smiled approvingly as if to say, "Well done, son!"

There was a hidden story behind that signed baseball. I was out for drinks one evening when my ride left early and I needed a ride back to Giants campaign headquarters. There was a threesome of older teens out front of the establishment. I bargained, "Hey kids, drive me over to University Plaza to the Friends of the Giants campaign headquarters and I'll give you all Giants shirts and caps." The boys agreed and drove me to headquarters where I showed them around and gave them the shirts and caps as promised.

With former Giants Owner, Bub Lurie

The next day I realized my Lurie-autographed baseball had disappeared–and I knew the culprits. Fortunately for me those little bastards weren't the sharpest tools in the shed and had signed the boosters' guestbook with their addresses and phone numbers. So I called them all and in my most authoritative voice told them a bullshit story about having taped his friends phone call using a high-tech recording system, and if they didn't return that baseball ASAP, they'd be screwed because the police would be right behind me if I didn't get that ball back. It wasn't long before they delivered the ball.

A SMOKE-FILLED ROOM

Like many graduates fresh out of college, I was in the usual *dazed and confused* state of mind with what to do with the rest of my life. Good fortune smiled on me when my sister Emmy was asked to manage the Santa Clara portion of the Giants Campaign. Unable to accept the assignment due to other business commitments, Emmy suggested her younger brother be considered. Now I had just started my dream job in development at Archbishop Mitty High School, my Alma Mater.

Soon after I was on a blind date at J.R. Chops, considered the City Hall Annex. Walking out after dinner, passing by the dank, dark banquet room, I saw the door fly open and so much smoke pour out I thought the room was on fire. Talk about smoke-filled rooms–this one was beyond the cliche! Developers were there, big time people, along with one of the Giants' key consultants. One stepped out, pointed at me and said, "We want to talk with you." Instantly I was dragged into the battle to bring professional sports to Santa Clara. And it got better when I was told, "We want to hire you to run the Santa Clara portion of the ballpark campaign." I was elated–my professional relationship with the Giants began.

We set up campaign headquarters downtown in the Old Quad. We decorated the vacant office from floor to ceiling with Giants memorabilia. I commandeered "Super Sue," mother of one of my friends, and an extraordinary artist, to design and paint a baseball hurling across the wall into the brand new ballpark that we were hoping to build. A grand opening party was attended by hundreds of fans, elected officials, Giants executives and a few superstars including All-Stars Will Clark and Matt Williams. I found this line of work extremely exciting!

HIRE ALL THE CONSULTANTS ... EXCEPT THOSE ON COCAINE

To oversee the campaign to bring the Giants to Santa Clara County, a team of consultants was needed. We were able to choose from the top consultants in the Bay Area, but the Giants were not enamored by any of them. One of the Giants advisers, a legendary figure in politics, opined comments to me as the candidates entered and exited the room: "That guy's a jerk! That guy's a jackass! Forget that guy." At last a consultant was hired. As campaign conductor whom we shall call "Casey Jones." My team's awesome volunteers were organized and effective in Santa Clara. In other South Bay cities the campaign strategy fell short. One guy on the opposing team deviously devised a light switch of Bob Lurie's face to demonstrate how the utility tax would raise the utility bill. Every time one turned on a light by flicking Bob's nose, one was reminded that he or she was paying for a stadium–outrageous!

The campaign funded by the Giants had a chance to hire some of the best consultants, but they didn't; the campaign hired an inexpensive consultant and got what they paid for in Casey Jones. Though I rather liked him, I was flat out pissed at his lack of organization. I reported that despite his proclamations, he didn't set up proper headquarters in collaborating cities, didn't monitor staff to the level necessary, didn't update the Committee with enough concrete progress.

(What I learned from that: *hire all the consultants!* With sufficient funds, why not have them all working for us, not against us. That's what we would do in the Niners campaign. We'd even hire people we didn't like; I even recommended an opponent–with whom I later became a friend. That was the winning tactic: put our egos aside, get locked and loaded.)

Two years later I was listening to the radio when I heard a news story that confirmed my earlier suspicions. This former political campaign strategist for the Giants campaign and for three San Jose mayors faced a maximum of nine years in prison for selling 'crack' cocaine to an undercover cop. Our conductor was indeed driving his train high on cocaine!

THE WILLIE MAYS BBQ

We planned a BBQ in Henry Schmidt Park in Santa Clara to bring out families in support of two ballot measures, Measure N and Measure G, to bring the Giants and a new Major League ballpark to Santa Clara. The higher-ups agreed to get us a celebrity, so I said, "Get us Willie Mays, in my mind the greatest baseball player of all time."

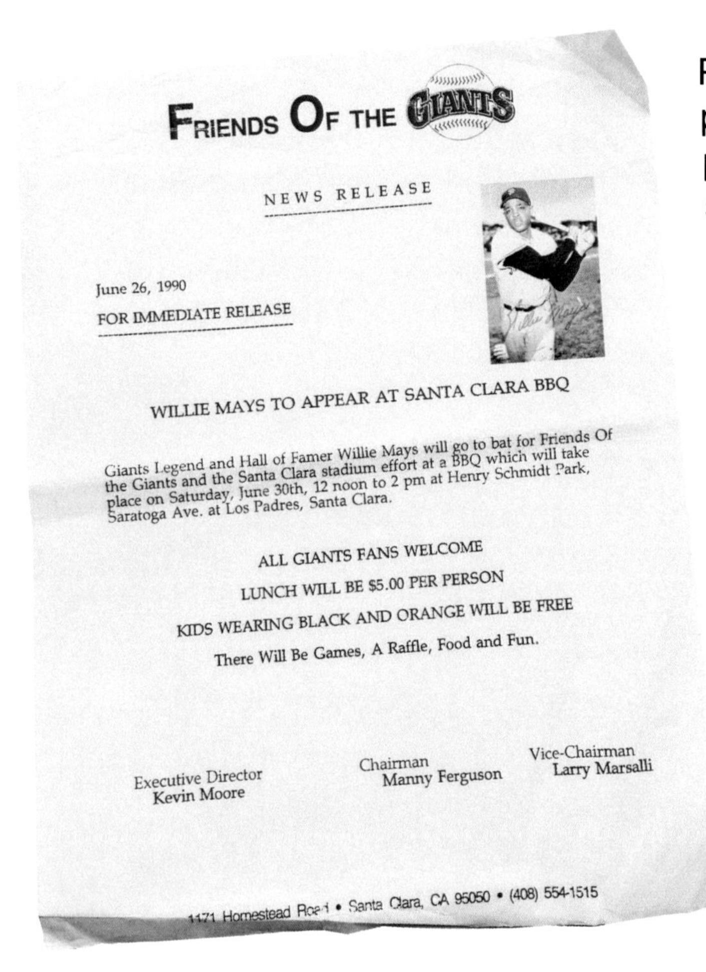

FRIENDS OF THE GIANTS

NEWS RELEASE

June 26, 1990

FOR IMMEDIATE RELEASE

WILLIE MAYS TO APPEAR AT SANTA CLARA BBQ

Giants Legend and Hall of Famer Willie Mays will go to bat for Friends Of the Giants and the Santa Clara stadium effort at a BBQ which will take place on Saturday, June 30th, 12 noon to 2 pm at Henry Schmidt Park, Saratoga Ave. at Los Padres, Santa Clara.

ALL GIANTS FANS WELCOME

LUNCH WILL BE $5.00 PER PERSON

KIDS WEARING BLACK AND ORANGE WILL BE FREE

There Will Be Games, A Raffle, Food and Fun.

Executive Director
Kevin Moore

Chairman
Manny Ferguson

Vice-Chairman
Larry Marsalli

1471 Homestead Road • Santa Clara, CA 95050 • (408) 554-1515

I drove to Candlestick Park the night before to get supplies. By this time I knew a lot of people at Candlestick Park. It seemed like I was living there, virtually attending games every night, I went to 61 games that year. Security let me drive my car into the stadium. I drove up the first ramp to the second level where vendors met me to load my car with peanuts. We filled the trunk then started filling the car. I had to rip open some of the boxes and throw bags of peanuts into open crevices. There were so many peanuts and accessories that I had to lower my convertible top to fit everything. On the drive back the weather was threatening, then misting, then it started to rain, and I was screwed. No way could I close my convertible top en route. I just hauled ass back to Santa Clara. At the campaign office I unloaded the peanuts and called it a wet night.

Next day the weather was flawless. I had beer donated for adults, and non-alcoholic beer, and sodas for kids. George who ran the snack bar at

Mitty High School came and gave away popcorn and hot dogs. I had hired a reggae band called Uprising, Their big guy named "Special K" was on stage doing jams, the music was rockin'. An estimated 500 people were in the park, the atmosphere was terrific, everything seemed perfect. Then Willie Mays was a no-show. We huddled up over what to do. The campaign secretary was frazzled, the Giants executive was despondent. One of the Giants consultants said, "Does anybody have a knife?" When asked why, he answered, "I want to slit my wrist." I too, was pissed, everything had been proceeding so well. Willie Mays–"where are you?" Families, the kids especially were getting restless. Then like a bolt of lightning, I was struck with an idea: Ronnie Lott lives down the street near Pruneridge Golf Course. If I go to his house, maybe, just maybe, I'll be lucky enough to convince him to come save the day. I had met Ronnie years before and on various occasions; he was the finest of gentlemen and great with kids.

I rushed to Ronnie's house, knocked on his door, it opened and there stood Ronnie. He looked like he had been sleeping and blinked, "Kev, what's up?"

"I'm screwed. I've got over 500 kids in the park and they've been waiting hours for Willie Mays to sign autographs and Mays is nowhere to be found." [I didn't know that the driver hired for Willie, instead of driving to the Saratoga exit in Santa Clara had exited on Saratoga/Sunnyvale Road and Willie was somewhere out near Shoreline Amphitheater!]

Ronnie validated his tired look.

'Kev, I was at my Roast last night and got in really late. Let me stick my head under water and I'll come over and sign some autographs."

Meanwhile, everybody at the park was restless, desperate to say the least. "Where the hell did Kev go?... Why did he leave?" My conscientious secretary was ready to have a heart attack. I returned to inform them and Mayor Eddie Souza what was in the works. Eddie wowed, "You just got

Ronnie Lott to come? My God, that's good work!"

Ronnie Lott pulled up on his Harley-Davidson motorcycle, driving slowly into Henry Schmidt Park, as cool as Fonzie ever was, and got off his bike. He had a 49ers jersey draped over his shoulder. I gave him a "Santa Clara Giants" baseball cap. Ronnie stepped up on stage, the reggae band wound down; he faced the crowd like he knew the game plan, and he said, "Team work is extremely important. When a team works for each other and for a common goal, greatness can and will happen....I have a trivia question for all of you out there....What team has won the last two Super Bowls?"

Ronnie Lott pulls up on his Harley to save the day at the Willie Mays BBQ!

A kid raised his hand and shouted, "the 49ers!"

And Ronnie pointed to the kid, "Right you are." He took the brand new football jersey off his shoulder and flung it out to the kid like Mean Joe Greene in the famous Coke commercial. After a few more words about the value of sports and teamwork, Ronnie stepped aside to sign autographs.

When it couldn't get any better, almost on cue, Willie Mays' car pulled up and out stepped the "Say Hey Kid." Now we've got Ronnie Lott signing autographs *and* Willie Mays. Ronnie was a class act. He greeted Willie with a big "Hello, Willie!" then stepped back and gave him center stage.

We had a four star event, and I had to thank Ronnie in particular. Before he left I had the Say Hey Kid autograph a sweatshirt: "If we build it, they will come"... and beneath the slogan: "To Ronnie Lott, from Willie Mays." Afterwards I took it over to Ronnie. Ronnie Lott, strong man that he is, one of the hardest hitters in NFL history, was truly touched. I, too, was deeply affected by the experience; I was hooked on working with the big leagues!

"...good barbeque is more complicated than you think."
- *Manish Dyal, American Actor*

MOORE. MOORE. MOORE. HOW DO YOU LIKE IT?

I was unable to attend an important Santa Clara City Council meeting. It was the night the council was planning to hire a team of financial experts to study the fiscal impact of building a ballpark in Santa Clara. They had an impressive list of top accounting firms to chose from.

So, I made a late-night call to Mayor Eddie Sousa."Hey Eddie, who did the City hire as the financial consultant?" Eddie, who normally has a very good sense of recall, could not remember the firm's name. I asked him, "Was it the accounting firm of Coopers and Lybrand?" Eddie said, "Yes, I am pretty sure it is." I responded with great enthusiasm for it was the firm where my older cousin, Nick Moore, played an integral role in management. Cousin Nick was bright, an extraordinary business leader, and a class-act.

Eddie replied, "Holy shit! You're running the Santa Clara portion of the campaign, your sister Emmy is a city planning commissioner who'll be reviewing plans for a possible rezoning for the ballpark, and we just hired your cousin as our financial analyst? Holy shit, if the press gets a hold of this, they could suspect a Moore Family conspiracy."

TAKING CARE OF BUSINESS

At the time of the ballpark campaign, I was driving my silver LeBaron convertible. This car seemed to drive itself in a repeated path which I tagged as the Triangle and the Toss. My triangular-shaped racetrack went from my "day job" in San Jose to the Santa Clara ballpark campaign office and then over to the Downtown San Jose campaign headquarters.

A campaign volunteer would often stand on the corner of South Market Street and Park Avenue in San Jose, and without stopping the vehicle, I would hastefully toss campaign documents out of the convertible and hope like heck the volunteer would catch them safely. Then, I'd hightail back to my fulltime job, without a moment to spare before the next meeting or deadline.

On one of those crazy days while scrambling to be in three places at once, I backed into a 16-foot lamp pole in the parking lot of my employer. I was okay and nobody got hurt, thank God. My Chrysler Lebaron did not fare as well and neither did my pocketbook. Cha-ching, a thousand dollar body shop repair bill.

I remember the last time I attempted the Triangle and the Toss. The song "Takin' Care of Business" by the rock group Bachman-Turner Overdrive was blaring on the radio and when I threw the roll of precinct maps to our volunteer at curbside, he made an awesome catch. It wasn't quite a Montana-to-Clark type of catch, but critical material was passed quickly so more precincts could be walked.

I'M TIRED

Between a demanding full-time job and attempting to run the Santa Clara portion of the ballpark campaign, sleep was seldom an option. It seemed as if I was working 24-7, some days 18 to 20 hours long. Those were crazy days and I was definitely sleep-deprived. This became pretty obvious late one evening. I mistakenly parked my car in my neighbor's driveway. No wonder my key wouldn't open the front door–it wasn't my house.

Later that week after a series of arduous work sessions, I was determined to prepare myself a carb-filled spaghetti dinner (i.e. comfort food). After completing my culinary assignment of pasta, veggies, and garlic bread, I was ready to dig in to my feast. But for some strange reason, instead, I picked up my plate and dumped it in the trash can. Yes, I tossed out the entire meal. That same night, instead of putting a carton of milk back in the fridge where it belonged, I placed it in an upper kitchen cabinet (one that rarely gets opened). I discovered the milk carton nearly two months later, and it looked like something from the movie Alien and smelled like a garbage dump. I was so, so tired.

ALL IN

Drastic situations require drastic measures, and the radical in me took three such actions. First, I took the initiative to persuade our leadership to get Giants owner Bob Lurie to pony up some extra cash. A $5,000 check came forth from Mr. Lurie and I printed 10,000 *Santa Clara Giants* t-shirts and 7,000 hats. Those t-shirts are now a collector's item!

Next, as a visible testimony to my allegiance to the Orange & Black campaign and to bring some good karma to the election, I had the house I was renting painted flourescent orange with black trim. The landlord was delighted to get his house painted for free until he saw the eye sore I'd created. When you're painting your house brown, no one helps. When you're painting your house flourescent orange, everybody helps. The job took just two hours with every neighborhood kid pitching in. Neighbors were not pleased, but it was temporary and surely succeeded in making a statement.

Despite all the efforts I was frustrated that the campaign was not doing enough. So, after one very long night of floor pacing in my Orange and Black house, I had convinced myself that we needed to release one more piece of kick-ass campaign material.

As the sun began to rise I found myself frantically designing that last compelling collateral piece. Next, I was off hand-delivering it to the campaign leadership for their review and approval. While they thoroughly enjoyed and editorially approved the piece, they ultimately vetoed it due to cost. There just weren't enough funds in the coffer. Of course, I couldn't let it go. So, after repeating yet another late night-into-morning perpetually pacing routine, I knew who I needed to talk with about this matter.

FACT: If the Giants move to Santa Clara, they will be called the SANTA CLARA GIANTS!

"Santa Clara has a nice ring to it!"

—Fay Vincent, Commissioner of Major League Baseball

TRAFFIC STUDIES ARE FAVORABLE!

"Most roads in the proposed stadium area have been widened due to Great America, Santa Clara Convention Center and surrounding businesses, thereby allowing for efficient traffic flow. Good roads make for a good traffic picture. Our report to the city of Santa Clara indicates a favorable analysis of the traffic we would encounter with the proposed stadium."

— Captain Terry Carmody, Santa Clara Police Dept.

"We should be quite proud of our City Staff for all their hard work in negotiating a good deal for our city. This is a once in a lifetime opportunity."

— Manny Ferguson, Ret. Chief of Police, City of Santa Clara

"If the children of Santa Clara could vote on this we would win by a landslide!"

— Kevin Tajii, age 12

ADDITIONAL INCOME FOR SANTA CLARA

"The bottom line is...this is a great investment for the City of Santa Clara. We will receive land lease payments of 4.3 million dollars yearly and this will increase by 25% every 5 years. This can go directly into the city budget for increase services for our residents."

— Don Von Raesfeld, Ret. City Manager, Santa Clara City Councilman

---

PLAY BALL SANTA CLARA GIANTS!

— Rita Kennedy, Senior Citizens Advisory Committee

"This will not only benefit our city economically. This could mean more money for our schools and educational programs.

— Don Callejon, Ret. Superintendant Santa Clara Unified School District

---

As a recent college graduate with nothing to my name but debt, I turned in desperation to my parents, "Mom, Dad, I need your help. I want to borrow $2000 to purchase a full-page *Santa Clara Giants* ad in the newspaper." Mom and dad looked at me in disbelief, "Kev, we'll have to sleep on this." Next morning there's an $2000 check on my dresser with a note from my mom: "If we build it, they will come." The ad featured Captain Terry Carmody of the Santa Clara Police Department, who had the guts to report a major traffic study that was favorable to traffic flow in the proposed stadium area, an empirical report that the City Manager refused to make public. Elements of that report were cited in the Niners' stadium campaign.

IF WE BUILD IT, THEY WILL COME

This first Santa Clara Giants Campaign landed two related ballot measures on the City's June election ballot. The first, Measure G which would fund the stadium project with a tax through a Joint Powers Authority (JPA) and relocate the team to Santa Clara as the "Santa Clara Giants." The second measure would approve 96 acres of city owned land to locate a ballpark for the San Francisco baseball organization

If We Build It They Will Come

Friends of the Giants, a local organization devoted to bringing the Giants to Santa Clara, recently opened their headquarters at University Plaza on the corners of Homestead and Jackson in Santa Clara. Santa Clara resident Kevin Moore, 25, (shown here standing between volunteers Dorothy Cassidy and Rosemary Wolf) is the volunteer, executive director charged with marshalling local forces in favor of a Mission City ballpark. Along with Giants' owner Bob Lurie and several as-yet unnamed players, Friends of the Giants will be hosting the grand opening of their office in Santa Clara with a celebration Wednesday, April 18 from 7 to 9 p.m. Music, food, refreshments and free admission to the 2,800 square feet office are offered to all Santa Clara residents and Giants' well-wishers. Moore, now director of development at Archbishop Mitty High School, first met Lurie when he was an 11-year old attending a Giants' exhibition game at Santa Clara University stadium.

Moore waved to Lurie outside the stadium and the team owner came over and signed his baseball.

The evening before the crucial election we held a Candlelight Vigil at the same Henry Schmidt Park. The vigil could be conceived as both the end of Candlestick Park and a luminous prayer to the gods for a Giants Stadium in Santa Clara. Throughout the campaign our slogan was lifted from *Field of Dreams: If we build it, they will come.* So I had this wild notion to contact Kevin Costner of said movie fame. Not hearing from Kevin Costner as he was filming *Dances with Wolves*, I reached out to his fellow cast members hoping one might provide some inspirational words akin to *Field of Dreams.* As the hour of the vigil drew near, suddenly the office fax machine began its lurching sound and what emerged was a letter from James Earl Jones.

To "All Baseball Fans"

As W.P. Kinsella writes in his book, Shoeless Joe: "I don't have to tell you that the one constant through the years has been baseball. America has been erased like a blackboard, only to be rebuilt again. But baseball has marked the time while America has rolled by like a procession of steamrollers. It continually reminds us of what once was, like an Indian-head penny in a handful of new coins." . . . I think this particular passage says it all. Let the Giants stay a constant in the Bay Area. If you build it–they will come!

Good Luck, James Earl Jones

IT WAS CLOSE

The Election Night Party was held at the old LeBaron Hotel on North First Street in San Jose. Sadly for me, Measure G went down in defeat, by a small margin. Now I had not drank a beer in three months while running the campaign, so tonight I was off the wagon sporting a three beer buzz. I was nervous when I saw Lloyd LaCuesta of Channel 2 News approach me for an interview. I had a Corona beer in my hand that I was not putting down! I positioned the beer behind my back as Lloyd pointed his microphone to my face and fired: "Now that the Giants initiative is going down in flames, as campaign director, what do you have to say?"

I looked up one more time at the returns, pointed with my free hand, and recounted to Lloyd, "But hey, look at Measure N, the land initiative, it's winning! The land approved here will open the door for future things." The land measure won by 510 votes. I had to believe that my full-page ad days before the election, having reached 21,000 households, might have made the difference...thanks to Mom & Dad!

December 19,1990

Dear Kevin,

I want to take this opportunity to thank you for your outstanding efforts in the recent ballpark initiative. It was close...

Robert A. Lurie, Chairman San Francisco Giants

ROCK BOTTOM

In the waning of this campaign, I'm drained and dispirited. At my place of work a sudden change in administration occurred. The new principal added to my development work the responsibility of Alumni Director; further, he disapproved my increasing role as campaign director. In order to continue my campaign leadership, I had to go rogue and work nighttime and off hours. Despite my best efforts in meeting my responsibilities and appeasing him, after the election it was clear he wanted to bring in his own people. In early November I resigned my position.

My relationship with my girlfriend of five years had sadly dissolved. I was not seeing much of family or friends. I was exhausted, fried, burnt out. Within weeks I came down with walking pneumonia. Thanksgiving rolled around and my parents invited me over for turkey dinner. I said "no." I did not want to be with people, did not want to do anything. I expressly did not want to see any ballgames, live or on TV. On Thanksgiving Day I ate a Swanson frozen turkey pot pie alone in my room. It was a low point in my life.

JENNY, I GOT YOUR NUMBER, BUT IT'S NOT 867-5309

A few weeks later, my friend's brother called me up and said, "Hey, let's go out to the Oasis downtown."

"No, I really don't want to go out."

"C'mon, Moore, you need to get out. We need to get you back on the horse. C'mon, man, let's go out."

We hit the Oasis night club but no one looked interesting enough to talk to or dance with. I was not in the mood for social drinking. I did not want to be there. So I suggested, "How about we head back to Santa Clara to The Hut (a bar) and Lord John's pub down near the University." The pub would often have a really good reggae band or otherwise played great music. And I lived nearby in case I needed to stumble home.

At Lord John's I sat back in the booth, listened to the music, stared into space. Joy and purpose had been sucked out of my life. Then I saw a pair of long sexy legs. Oh my God! It was a vision of heaven. I refocused and became enamored of her long brown hair and striking green eyes and her aqua-blue outfit. I jumped up and my friend says, "Whoa, Moore, what's up?" I pointed to the beauty, he nodded, "Okay, yeah, I see."

The music was so loud you couldn't hear a spoken word, but the song lyrics spoke clearly to me: *I'll stop the world and melt with you.* I rose, walked over to her and asked, "Would you care to dance?" She turned around, looked at me, and I thought I heard her say, "No, thanks." I started to walk away.

Photo courtsey of Joe Antuzzi

"Hey," she said, "I thought you wanted to dance."

I turned back around and escorted her to the dance floor. After a few songs I bought her a drink. It was hot so we sat outside and started to talk. All I knew was that I wanted her. I was uplifted. Here was someone I could live for after the hell I'd been through. She wrote her number on the back of my Parks & Recreation business card. We started dating, I was back in the game. Now I'm six-foot-three so I liked that she was tall; my buddies nicknamed her "Five-Ten Jen" though she was actually five-foot-eleven.

He leads me beside still waters; he restores my soul. He leads me in paths of righteousness ... Psalm 23:2

2nd Quarter

IF AT FIRST YOU DON'T SUCCEED…

After defeat of the ballot measure (to bring the Giants to Santa Clara) dashed Bob Lurie's hope for a new ballpark, he started shopping the team around. While Florida showed strong interest, his own cold and windy baseball stadium–recall the Croix de Candlestick!–depressed attendance. As early as 1990, Safeway magnate Peter Magowan began assembling a partnership team to try to purchase the Giants from Mr. Lurie. In November of that year, I received a voice message from Peter Magowan, followed up by a phone call from his secretary, asking to meet with him and the Santa Clara Stadium Association assembled earlier. Peter was a class act and I was pleased to be on "stand-by" pending their negotiations to purchase the team. Anticipating my participation in bringing the Giants to the South Bay, I renewed my involvement in attending Giants games and keeping in the loop with the prospective new owners.

HOUSTON, WE HAVE A PROBLEM

A former Santa Clara City official offered me a Luxury Suite for a game at Candlestick Park. When he asked if I wanted the luxury box my response was automatic, "Yes! For sure, all right, thank-you!" We had worked closely on the failed attempt to bring the Giants here and could be working the angle again. Soon I was dialing a couple buddies for a boys' night out; one asked if he could bring the girl he was dating. I knew her to be an absolute doll, an all-American girl. "Yeah, okay, bring her along."

In the suite drinking beers and enjoying the game, the urge came for several of us to relieve ourselves. We excused ourselves from my buddy and his girlfriend and headed for the restroom. We delayed returning, strolling the rafters and picking up another round of beers. Upon our return security guards were standing in front of our box looking through a curtain that looks into the suite. "What's the problem, officers?"

Rather than answer us they said, "You're going to have to come with us to the Security Office." Glancing beyond the guards we too saw through the window: my buddy and his All-American girl freshening themselves up, shall we say. Apparently what began as a kissing session went well past second base! Security made no bones about being highly offended and dragged us down to their second floor office. There behind the desk was a lady I knew and liked, though she had a reputation as a tough cookie. Her last name was Houston and all I kept thinking was "Houston, we've got a problem." She said she'd have to report this *incident*. I figured that meant the cops, the whole nine yards; and we were up shit-creek without a paddle. Moreover, we were in the luxury box of our former highest ranking city official–a political faux pas. The story was not going to end well. Add to this dire situation that another buddy past the three-beer buzz started getting cocky.

My buddy with the sheepish grin on his face, still tucking in his shirt, turned to our other friend and told him "Shut the f-- up. Let Kevin do the talking." So here I was confronted with Ms. Houston. I flashed back to my Catholic school days and means of dealing with the nuns, but what might have charmed Sister Ann Elizabeth wouldn't get far with this woman.

"Ms. Houston," I pleaded, "before you have these two carted off to jail or publicly humiliated, may I make one final request. Allow me to go down to my car and get that 'Santa Clara Giants' jacket that you so wanted a while back. Now I realize that you've got to do your job and do what you think is right, but while I'm getting you that jacket, maybe you can sort this thing out."

So two of us hauled ass down to the car. Out of breath we grabbed the jacket I fortunately had in the trunk and hurried back up to the security office. I handed Ms. Houston this gorgeous orange & black Giants jacket. Her eyes twinkled like it was Christmas morning. She then explained to us that she thought the situation over, and there really wasn't much to report. But we were warned to be on our best behavior when in her stadium.

She stood up, leaned across her desk, and gave me a hug. We left immediately. All the way to the car I prayed: "Holy Mary, Mother of God, pray for us sinners, now and at the hour of our death. Amen."

Statue of the Blessed Virgin Mary at
Shrine of Our Lady of Peace
Roman Catholic Church,
Santa Clara, California

Photo by W.J. Parolini

THE JUDAS STORY

Santa Clara's re-elected mayor was Eddie Souza with whom we were again working to literally *Save the Giants* from leaving the Bay Area. We were fairly confident we could attract the team. To this end my bedroom walls were covered on three sides with strategic notes, news articles, letters and pictures pertaining to this second Giants effort. My room resembled an FBI office in *Criminal Minds* covered with photos strung together to solve a crime!

During that period I received a phone call at 6:04am from the *Santa Clara Valley Weekly*. I was not an early riser; no one should have to think and answer questions before 10, or at least before caffeine after a night of drinking. So I was in bed trying to get a grip on the phone call. The reporter was trying to inform me that he knew for sure "one guy on the Santa Clara Council is *not* on your team on this stadium issue." I didn't know who he meant but certainly wanted to find out. Thinking as best I could in the pre-rational hour I said: "I know, but it's not the oldest councilmen with the most clout; so I wouldn't worry about him too much." The reporter responds, "Shit, so then you do know who it is" and gave his name away.

Later that day I did some research, made some phone calls and confirmed that the *traitor* the reporter was talking about was a councilman nicknamed the "Lizardman"–tagged for his slime green body-painted get-up to rouse spirit at Santa Clara Broncos basketball games, where he charged up and down the stands raising cheers to fever levels while spilling fans' popcorn in the process.

Come to find out this councilman was simultaneously working with the City of San Jose to lure the Giants. I reported to Mayor Souza that Lizardman was working behind our backs and that I'd have a talk with him. Eddie countered, "No, leave it to me, I'll handle this." After the Council meeting that week Eddie summoned the Lizardman into the backroom. He asked the man to hold out his hand and handed him a knotted handkerchief containing silver coins. Lizardman was speechless.

A few days later an Op-ed piece by Lizardman titled *My Giant Debate* appeared in the *Santa Clara Valley Weekly*:

"In the winter of 1989, I joined the Santa Clara County Stadium Task Force...a group of well-respected regional leaders dedicated to the effort of attracting the San Francisco Giants to Santa Clara County. Central to the effort...was to build a major league baseball stadium.... In the fall of 1990 the majority of Santa Clarans said "Yes" (to building a stadium on city-owned land).... However, the (same) majority said "No" (to pay for the stadium utilizing a utility tax).

"At this time, Eddie Souza was re-elected mayor of Santa Clara, and was dedicated to bringing in the Giants. Susan Hammer was elected mayor of San Jose, and buoyed by a utility tax, stated San Jose would be their new home.

"However, when pursuing the Giants on behalf of Santa Clara, I am not personally competing with my council associates in San Jose. I view both municipalities' efforts as mutually beneficial."

As a resident of Santa Clara my reaction to Lizardman was: "are you f-- kidding me?!?" Twice in the month of July '91 I received voice messages from said councilman asking for Giants campaign updates and proclaiming his desire for involvement. I was a good friend to the Lizardman but it was now clear that council members did not trust him and felt his lack of loyalty to the City was flat out unacceptable.

"What will you give me if I deliver him to you?" And they paid him thirty pieces of silver... Matt 26:15

JUNE 1992. Giants fail in their bid to build and locate in San Jose. Despite the promising passage of a utility tax the previous year, the San Jose vote to actually build a stadium in Santa Clara County was a blowout, almost 58% against. Without knowing for certain at this time, this election was the end of public voting to build a baseball stadium in the South Bay.

WHO WILL TAKE A CHECK?

My love life renewed with Five-Ten-Jen by my side, and I was back in the game. New management and unending faith led me to believe that the Giants could as yet settle in my hometown. Wanting to impress the Peter Magowan ownership group with my dedication, on short notice I decided to travel down to LA for a Giants vs Dodgers game. Jen and I cruised down Hwy 101 in my silver LeBaron convertible with the southern California sun shining down on us and we drove direct to Chavez Ravine, home of the Dodgers. There we encountered one small problem–I had no tickets. Now I did have reservations at the Dodgers VIP Club thanks to my connected friend "JP" but no way into the stadium. With the National Anthem already echoing, I sought out the scalpers to buy some tickets quick. Only now there's a bigger problem–I've neglected to bring any cash–I will have to see if I can get a ticket scalper to take a check!

Drawing by Gina Moore

I asked a couple of Dodgers fans, "Excuse me, Dodger fans, where's a good place to get scalper tickets?" and they pointed out the best place. I'm dressed in a sports coat and tie for the VIP Club as I headed over toward the scalpers who quickly circled 'round (dare I say like birds of prey), a group of about 20.

I raised my voice and said, "Hey, I'm going to ask you guys something that's completely asinine. You're not going to want to do this, but I'm going to ask it anyway. See that beautiful girl standing next to that Chrysler?" They nodded and gawked. "I want to impress her. We've driven down from Santa Clara. It's a perfect day. But I have no cash on me and I want to buy your best tickets. So who will take a check? You can call the bank, you can do

The Chronicle presents

Profile of a Giant Fan

KEVIN MOORE

This week the team jacket for Giants' Greatest Fan goes to Kevin Moore of Santa Clara because he:

- Painted his house fluorescent orange
- Spent his last $2,000 on an ad for the Santa Clara ballpark campaign
- Talked a scalper into taking a check at Dodger Stadium for seats behind the Giants' dugout
- At 5 years old walked home 3 miles from a Giant's exhibition game because his sister left early and he wouldn't.
- Had a childhood hero – Bob Lurie, who saved the Giants from moving...

LAST CHANCE!

Enter the "PROFILE OF A FAN" Contest.

Tell us why you are the Giants' greatest fan in 100 words or less, and send your entry, with a photograph of yourself, to: Giants Fan, San Francisco Newspaper Agency, 814 Mission St., Rm. 602, San Francisco, CA 94103. Include your name, address and phone no. Six winning profiles will appear in the Sporting Green, and the successful fans will...

WIN A PERSONALIZED GIANTS' JACKET!

San Francisco Chronicle

The Bay Area's Leading Newspaper.

whatever you want to feel sure. I know it's completely insane, but I'm hoping one of you guys is crazy enough to trust this face."

The scalpers look at one another in disbelief, there's a pregnant pause before they broke out laughing. We bonded right then and there. One of the guys cussed, "Shit, I trust this guy's face. I can't believe I'm doing this, but I'm going to take a f-- check."

Another scalper chimed, "I can't tell you why, but I'd trust this guy too." I write the scalper a check for $120.

With tickets in hand, we entered Dodger Stadium's main gate, bypassed our seats and headed up to the Stadium VIP Club where we had reservations. I was praying to run into anyone of the Giants' brass, and *bingo*, outside the club was Peter Magowan, Giants' owner. We exchanged a quick "hello, good to see you down here in LA; let's hope it's a good series; I'll look forward to talking more with you soon." Just the news I wanted to hear. I shook his hand, then Jen and I entered the Stadium Club.

On a visit years ago with family friends I remembered JP pulling out his Union 76 gas station credit card to pay the tab. Jen and I had just finished a fabulous dinner, draining the last drops from a magnum of champagne. Upon receipt of the check I pulled out my Union 76 gas card. "Kev, that's your gas station card" said Jen caringly, not wanting to be embarrassed a second time for having no cash.

"Yeah, I know!" I boasted without batting an eye. The waiter took the card and returned with the receipt. Unless you knew that there was a 76 gas station in the parking lot and that Dodger owners, the O'Malleys were friends of Union 76 corporate executives, you'd never have tried this trick. All in all, I thought I was pretty cool. I was starting to discern the way the world really worked.

DODGER STADIUM ... ANGELS IN THE PARKING LOT

A couple years later my relationship with a girlfriend to whom I had been totally faithful was suddenly in question. One of my best buddies Paul was also having a hard time in a relationship that was hanging by a thread. So it was time to take a road trip, a Giants-Dodgers season-ending series. This was a showdown for the Western Division title. On the way down to the ballpark, I phoned the Giants VP Larry Baer because he had said "Let me know if you need tickets down in LA." Not connecting with Larry as he was in the air, my default was once again–the ticket scalpers! "Hey guys, remember me, I wrote you a check last time–the bank cashed it, right? Well, this time I have cash, and I need to get seats very close to where the Giants owners' seats are located.

"Hey, I remember you. Yeah, I can help. You're gonna have to talk to my cousin Juan up in the stadium, but here's what we do. Come tomorrow, we'll get you some cheap crappy tickets, third deck seats. You buy 'em, get in the park, then meet this guy up on the third deck and he'll hook you up. Bring the cash, no check this time!"

Next day we showed up, got our scalped tickets, and met Juan on the third deck inside the men's bathroom. "Here's the deal. You guys give me $50 per VIP ticket and I'll get you right behind the owners' seats." That sounded too good to be true, but the scalpers had given me a fair deal before. So we each gave Juan $50 cash and he took us to the escalator. "Now, you're gonna meet Hector on the second floor, he'll tell you what to do next."

On the second floor, Hector said, "Take this escalator down to the first floor. You'll see a white line, stand behind it. You'll meet Julio, and Julio is going to hook you guys up."

So off we went blindly and muttering to ourselves that all we've got in hand are third deck tickets. We descended to the first floor, found and stood behind a white line. This guy came up to us, "I'm Julio. Follow me." He walked us down into lower deck VIP box seats right behind Peter Magowan, Willie Mays, and Bobby Thomson!!! We scored big time!

Later, when we walked up to get a Dodger Dog and a beer, we ran into Larry Baer. "Hi Kev, got your message. I had tickets waiting for you."

"No problem, Larry, we're okay." When we descended the stairs to our seats, Larry couldn't help but comment, "Gentleman, you've got great seats, you must have some great connections down here."

"Yeah, I know some people down here," I said wearing a smile while thinking, "God bless Juan and Julio and Hector!"

One of my best buddies, Paul Miller

We had gotten ourselves a room at the Giants hotel. For the last game of the series we wanted to revisit the Stadium Club where I once again would pull out my 76 card to everyone's amazement. We were joined by my college friend, Pat McBride, living in Orange County. Required Stadium Club dress was jackets and ties of which we failed to inform my friend before he met us at the hotel. When he arrived in casual clothes, after an "oh, shit, oh, shit," we said, "that's okay, you can wear some of our clothes." Now my buddy and I are both six-foot-three and my friend Pat is five-foot-six at best. Having donned our formal clothes, standing before the hotel room mirror Pat moaned, "I look like a clown."

My buddy and I assured him, "No, no you don't." But then we looked at each other, grinning and nodding "Yes, yes, he does look like a clown."

We watched the game and had more than a few beers, certain the Dodgers would hold on for the win. I turned to Pat and with a straight face blurted out, "If the Giants lose, we're coming back tonight to chainsaw those palm trees behind the outfield." Knowing just how crazy we could be, my college buddy was abuzz. He actually thought we were going to cut down those palm trees. He could already hear the chainsaws buzzing!

Exiting the stadium with my friends, my eyes caught sight of these two beautiful girls, one looked like Mary Ann from Gilligan's Island, the other could have been Christie Brinkley's little sister. They were standing next to a body builder, but I yelled across to them and waved. The girls seemed to be receptive. My buddy whispered, "Kev, that guy they're hanging out with is huge. You want to get us killed?"

I said not to worry and with my six beer courage I walked over to the bodybuilder, put my arm around his shoulder and asked, "Whichever one of these angels is your girlfriend, she's absolutely beautiful."

He answered casually, "Na, they're just friends."

I professed to him, "I love you, man, you just made my day." And to these two beautiful angels I said jokingly, "Did it hurt? Did it hurt when you fell from heaven?" Then I added seriously, "Do you girls want to come back to our hotel and party with the Giants?" They actually took our phone number and hotel information.

As we walked away, my buddy uttered, "Those girls are never coming to the hotel for us guys."

A while later we returned to the hotel, and right there in the lobby were Giants All-Stars Jeff Kent and Matt Williams. I caught an elevator with my buddy Paul, and who else rode up with us but Barry and Bobby Bonds. Barry Bonds was a superstar at this point. I turned toward them both and opined, "You're one of the greatest!" Barry smiled his trademark smile, thinking that I spoke my comment to him. But directing my focus to his father, Bobby, I followed, "Bobby, I was a big fan of yours, even had my mom make me a jersey with ironed-on letters B-O-N-D-S on the back." Bobby's face lit up. I realized he must have often felt overshadowed by his son. Then I turned to Barry who was actually smiling and I stuck it to him, "Barry, we went to Mitty High. You went to our rival Serra. You suck." For a split second he hesitated, then we all broke up in laughter.

After time in the room I headed down to the lobby. Folks were getting players' autographs. I didn't care about current players' autographs; but there was an old timer whose signature I wanted badly–Bobby Thomson of the "Shot Heard 'Round the World" fame; the guy who hit the home run evoking the famous call: "The Giants win the pennant, the Giants win the pennant, the Giants win the pennant"–over the Brooklyn Dodgers no less. And I got Bobby Thomson's autograph on my game ticket. I was in baseball heaven's Hall of Fame! It was truly amazing to see a sports legend from your baseball card days suddenly materialize before your very eyes.

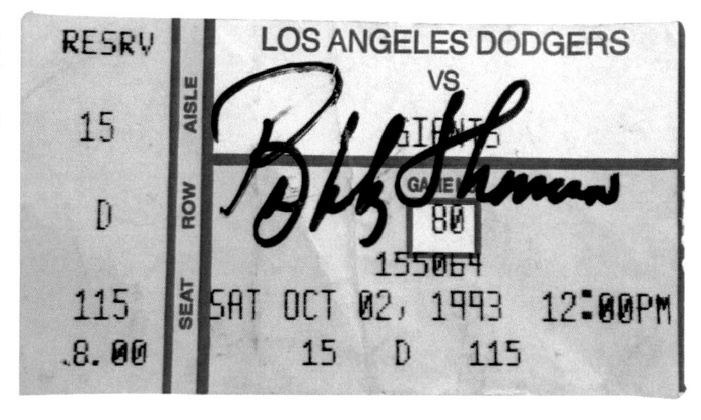

Suddenly I detected the sweet fragrance of perfume while feeling a gentle tap on my shoulder. I spun around to see the two Southern California angels standing in front of me. We ascended up the elevator to our hotel room. When these gorgeous women followed me in the door, my buddy Paul went flush-faced into shock. The darling duet echoed, "So, you guys wanted to party with us?"

Paul quickly came to his senses and emoted, "I can't believe you two showed up!"

"Well here we are." We could not have believed we were lucky enough to party with these two beautiful ladies: "Let's play ball!" We partied till the sun came up and remembered this night long after the Boys of Summer were gone.

GIANTS LEAVE THEIR HEART IN SAN FRANCISCO

Peter Magowan and Larry Baer always treated me well and with respect. So they invited me to their Executive Office at Candlestick Park, they had news to share with me personally. I took Five-Ten Jen along and while driving north to The Stick I tried not to be distracted by her presence, especially her long shapely legs, a distraction more dangerous than texting. I dropped Jen off at her internship in San Francisco and headed to The Stick. To my great disappointment, Peter and Larry informed me that the Santa Clara talks were terminating; and they were determined to build a new stadium in San Francisco. They thanked me for all my efforts and asked for my understanding and support of their new plan for a China Basin ballpark. I swallowed my pride and assured them of my full allegiance.

Flash forward to April 11, 2000. I received a personal invitation to attend Opening Day in the Giants' new San Francisco home, PacBell Park. I was still aggrieved with all the efforts that had gone into campaigns to build the Giants a ballpark in the South Bay, but I put on a happy face and attended the game. Once inside the stadium I realized and reconciled this *was* meant to be home for the Giants–what a beautiful Ballpark on the Bay!

THE SCHOTT HEARD 'ROUND THE WORLD

Recovering from broken dreams and broken relationships, I was back in the Islands living on the beach at Diamond Head, happy to have returned. I was the picture of "hang loose," growing my hair long, writing, working on a screenplay, teaching school, walking Diamond Head every day. I was living the dream. Then I heard it first through the media, then a phone call from Gary Hansen, a former councilman who had worked on the stadium issue. "Did you hear that Schott bought the Athletics and wants to move them to the South Bay?"

The Business Journal

• SERVING SAN JOSE AND SILICON VALLEY •

A's may play ball with Silicon Valley

San Jose, Santa Clara vying to build new stadium for baseball team

BY LYNN GRAEBNER
Staff writer

Don't uncork the champagne just yet, but plans for a big-league ballpark in Silicon Valley have quietly taken a step forward. A group of high-profile individuals in Santa Clara County calling themselves the Santa Clara Stadium Association say the Oakland A's have reviewed their group's proposal to build a new ballpark for the team in the city of Santa Clara.

WHAT'S A STADIUM NAME WORTH? SEE PAGE 45

Meanwhile, San Jose officials are batting numbers around with the team, exploring the possibility of a ballpark there.

But no one is building anything until Major League Baseball blesses a deal. Right now it's unclear where those discussions stand. Richard Levin, a spokesman for baseball Commissioner Bud Selig, said, "I'm not aware of any talks. But that doesn't mean that they aren't going on."

Another potential foul ball is that the San Francisco Giants already hold territorial rights to Santa Clara County and could litigate to keep the Oakland A's out.

While the A's won't acknowledge talks with groups from the cities of Santa Clara or San Jose, team officials say discussions to extend its lease at Network Associates

— SEE OAKLAND ON PG 45

Larry Stone, Gary Hansen and Kevin Moore (left to right) of the Santa Clara Stadium Association have devised a plan that doesn't involve public subsidy.

"I know."

"When are you coming back? You need to get on a plane."

"No, I'm not coming back."

Steve Schott, a Santa Clara native, together with Ken Hoffmann purchased the Oakland Athletics from Walter Haas, Jr. My mom was a good friend of Schott's mom; they attended Church at the Carmelite Monastery. Schott hinted that chances were good to move the team south. So I did come back and we started rolling on this new effort to lure the A's to Santa Clara. We had information from the Giants campaigns, surveys, traffic and weather studies, studies of studies, all this background; I was glad I had saved it. After some preliminary meetings, Gary set up a big one at the Hyatt. This meeting had the whole group back together, the who's who, the old guard, including Don Von Raesfeld, former mayor Gary Gillmor, Eddie Souza; Earl Carmichael,

Director of Parks & Recreation, as well as long time stadium advocates Larry Stone and Dr. Elliot Lepler. The lunch bill was high. I was glad Eddie picked up the tab; I sure didn't have much money.

WHEN KEVIN MOORE TALKS...

At a subsequent meeting, it was determined that an updated feasibility study was needed for Santa Clara to be credible. Now imagine being in a room where nobody gives a crap what you're saying. You're with people who think they're superior to you and don't give you the time of day. You're in a movie scene where the camera moves slowly away and you fade smaller and smaller into the background. So these big shots were talking, "We're thinking maybe we can get PricewaterhouseCoopers to help us out. We know some people there."

Now I've been faded out, out the window, over the parking lot, over the Sloughs of Alviso, forgotten. But from my corner seat my voice rose: "My cousin works for PricewaterhouseCoopers."

The guy turned his head to look across the room to me. "Excuse me," he said.

"My cousin works for PricewaterhouseCoopers," I repeated.

"Oh, in the San Jose office."

"No, in their New York Office. Nick Moore."

He perked up measurably, "Your cousin is the number one guy at Pricewaterhousecoopers?"

Next thing you know, I'm leading the meeting, everyone is listening attentively to me. On the way out one of the Santa Clara Stadium Association board members said to me "Kev, one minute no one is listening to you and the next minute you're E.F. Fuckin Hutton."

FACE PAINTED FAXING AT PRICE WATERHOUSE COOPER

Meetings with the Athletics continued. I was coordinating with Ed Alvarez, a consultant for the A's, a great guy who had worked for the 49ers. I was gathering documentation relative to a potential Oakland move to Santa Clara. This one day I was painting a house I had recently bought and rushing to get done because other repairs were to follow. I was not a good painter. When I removed the painters' tape and plastic drop-clothes paint drippings poured down on my face like a waterfall. I was about to clean up when under the paint-soaked newspapers the phone rang. Ed Alvarez told me it was critical that I get him the documents no later than 5 o'clock. I've got paint on my face and clothes but don't have time to change. I hauled ass over to his office in San Jose. It's locked. Every time I had ever been there, somebody was always there. Time was ticking; I calculated that I had some seven minutes to get him the needed information. I exited to the street looking wildly for a Kinko's when to my surprise I see a PricewaterhouseCoopers San Jose office.

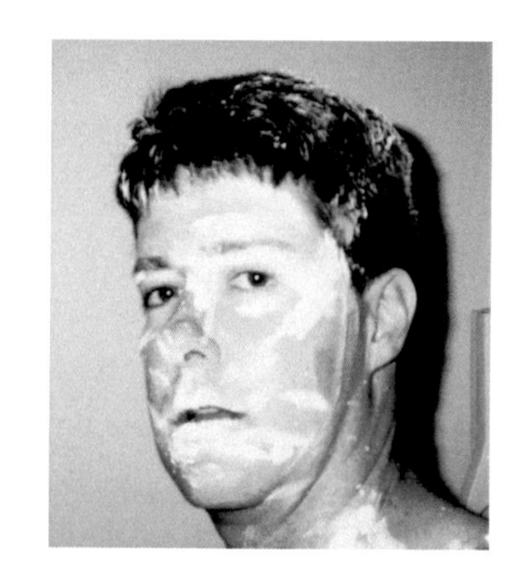

I ran across the street, barreled through the door. The receptionist looked like she'd seen a ghost or maybe a crazy man loosed of his straight jacket. "Can I help you?"

"Yeah, I need to use your fax machine."

"Sir, we cannot let anyone off the street come in and use our fax machine."

"I can understand, but my cousin works for your company."

"And who's your cousin?"

"Nick Moore."

"Oh, then in that case, fax what you need." She assisted me with the fax, then realized: "I should ring the head partner in the office, just to let him know." The San Jose partner, a Mitty High School alum, looked nothing like me at this point. He advanced down the hall in a suit so fine I felt like I was a child's paint-by-number portrait.

"Mr. Moore, come on back to my office," he said. I carefully sat my butt down, hoping I wouldn't get paint on his couch or coffee table. "What are you working on that brought you here with such urgency?"

"We're working to bring the A's to Santa Clara."

"That's interesting."

"Yeah, we'll see how it goes, but we could use your help. How about a preliminary financial analysis for starters?"

"You may need to call your cousin for that."

"No, I'd prefer that you make the call; this could be good for your San Jose office."

The San Jose partner talked to Nick and out of that conversation not only did we get the preliminary financial analysis, but PwC prepared a second financial analysis and even sent their top Sports Management executives from their Texas division to a council meeting. We now had the credibility of PricewaterhouseCoopers, one of the top accounting firms in the world.

"All you need to paint is a few tools, a little instruction, and a vision in mind."
–Bob Ross, American Painter

EVERYTHING OLD IS NEW AGAIN

There was yet another meeting set up by Gary Hansen, now Chairman of the Santa Clara Ball Park Association, helping lead the charge with Oakland Athletics and Co-Owner Steve Schott to bring the A's to Santa Clara. I was overlooked in the invitations to attend and was displeased. Swallowing my pride in an attempt to be a solid team member of the Association, I nonetheless called Gary on his cell as he was heading over to meet with Schott to discuss a parking diagram I designed. "Good luck with Schott, Gary. If you have questions on the parking diagram, I'm available by phone."

Hansen was always cool and full of charm and wit, but not now, he sounded quite agitated. "Kev, I'm in Schott's parking lot and I completely forgot to bring the parking diagram."

"No problem, Gary, happy to retrieve it; where's it at?"

"My real estate office on First Street."

Having been to Gary's office numerous times, I knew that it was a good 15 minute drive from my office to his. I was back driving my 1968 Firebird but had not pushed the pedal to the metal in the Bird since high school, but that 400 horsepower engine did not let me down. I made it to Gary's office in 9 minutes, grabbed the huge parking poster glued to a large piece of cardboard backing, and again putting pedal to metal. I made it to Schott's office with 20 seconds to spare before he entered the conference room. I stayed for the presentation – a huge success! Leaving the meeting Gary was smiling ear to ear; from then on I was always invited.

That parking diagram came in handy some twelve years later in initial meetings with the 49ers when they requested parking information on our Santa Clara site. I found it in Hansen's office behind a huge filing cabinet; the edges were curled and cobwebs that hung from both sides were as thick as those in the Munster's mansion on 1313 Mockingbird Lane.

I grabbed the parking poster diagram and took it to Kinko's at 3 a.m. the morning of the Niners meeting. The Kinko's manager performed emergency surgery on it and had it looking brand new. The 49ers were impressed!

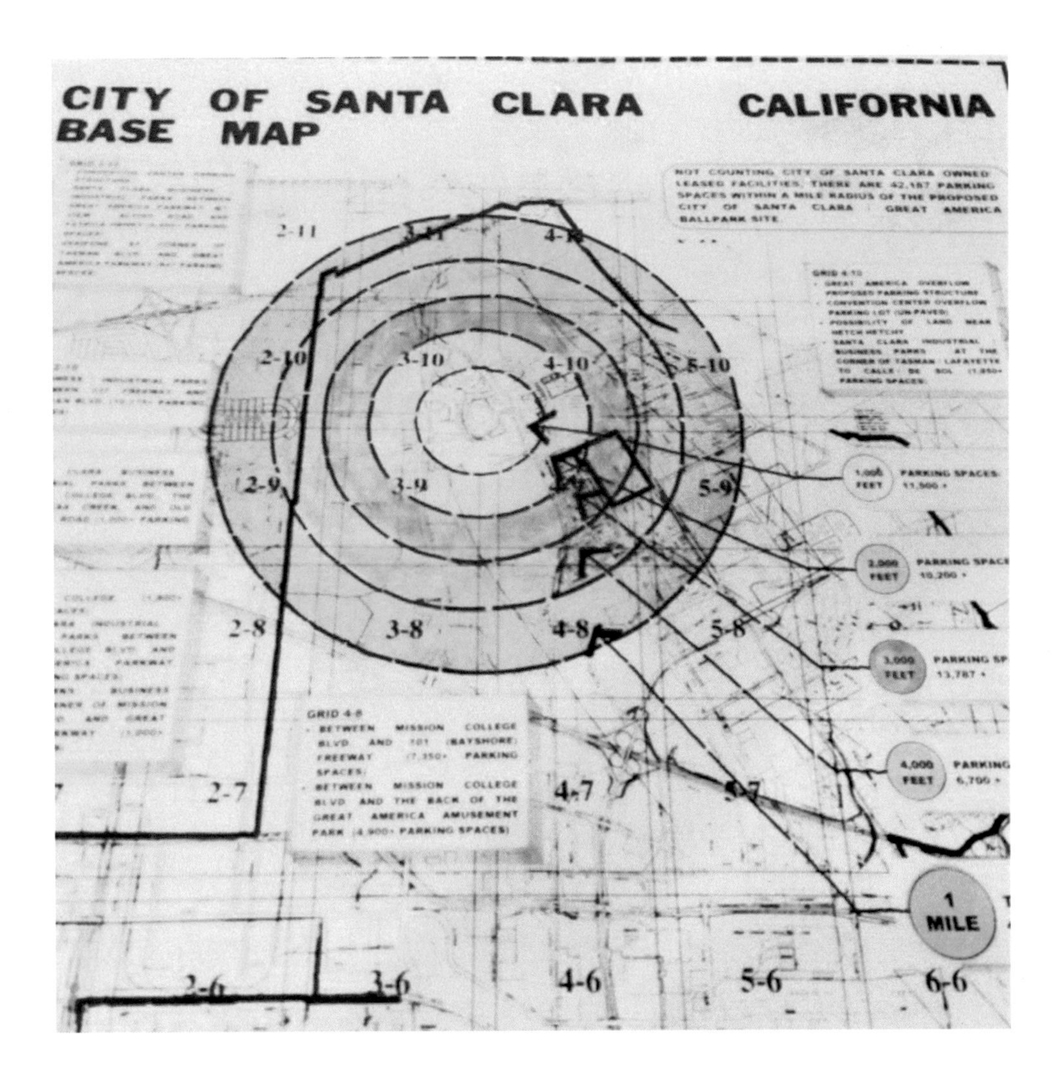

HOLY TOLEDO, IT'S COLD OUTSIDE

I took my dad up to Oakland for the first game of the Athletics' season and an opening night celebration. We were special guests of owner Steve Schott and our seats were sweet. When I unexpectedly ran into a Santa Clara City Council member, he said to me that by some mix-up his seats were in the second to last row of the third deck. He was really distraught!

It was bitter cold at the Coliseum that night. Dad was freezing so I decided to see how Steve Schott would respond to a big favor on a big night. I boldly took Dad up to the A's executive's offices on the second deck and asked the secretary to call Steve Schott's owner's box. You could tell she was not excited to disturb the team owner on this important night. I believe my Dad's smiling Irish eyes gave her the courage to make the call. This being opening night, celebrities and dignitaries demanded her attention, yet I was having her calling into the owner's box on my behalf. A few seconds later the secretary passed me the phone, Steve Schott was on the other end of the line. I said, "Hello, Steve, it's Kevin Moore. I'm here with my father, Jack, and he's freezing his you-know-what off." Without hesitation Steve invites us up to his owner's box and dad and I were living the dream. Dad sipped a hot chocolate like it was an expensive glass of wine. Dad's smile was absolutely priceless.

THE LAST SUPPER

After surviving that cold night dad graciously passed on accepting any A's night game invitations for the next two years until one night I begged him to brave the cold one MOORE time! In the words of former A's announcer Bill King, "HOLY TOLEDO" – this night was by far one of the coldest nights ever at the Oakland Coliseum; it was a bone chilling, a Candlestick Park kind of night. My Dad was bundled up like an Eskimo, but it kept getting colder and colder, inning by inning. Then the light bulb goes on over my head as I watched dad rubbing his hands together like he was making a wish on a magic lantern. I thought to walk up to Schott's owner's box for an encore; so that's just what the old, cold man and I did. The security guard knew me pretty well by this time, was welcoming and asked, "Are you Mr. Schott's guest tonight?" Dad and I shook our heads yes. The door was opened and we were in the owner's box once again… except that Steve Schott was in Washington D.C. accepting an award from the President of the United States – a recipient of George H. Bush's 1000 Points of Lights Award.

So now we were in the owner's box with Steve's co-owner Ken Hoffman, who I had only met once before. I turned to my dad and said, "Dad, look like we belong here, get into line and start grabbing food and a brew and meet me at a seat in the back." I went over and started talking to some of the A's executives who were chatting with guests. I looked back and saw Dad grab a fancy monogramed china plate and load it with food like it was his very own last supper. The plate was overflowing with every food item in the place, and he topped it with a huge carmel apple. Seeing him balancing the mound of goodies I could only think, "Oh my God, I hope he doesn't drop anything on the floor of this beautiful luxury suite."

Dad sat down, not in the back of the suite but up front in the best seats, right next to the Bishop of Oakland. I thank God that Dad is a fantastic storyteller who could carry an interesting conversation with anybody. So Dad and the Bishop of Oakland started exchanging stories. A bonus to his storytelling was that Dad had grown up in Oaktown and attended St. Joseph's of Alameda. After a couple innings and a couple more beers, it was clear that we were ordained to be there. Then suddenly Co-Owner Hoffman confronted me as I grabbed for another brew, "Oh no," I thought, "Dad and I are going to get the boot."

But Ken said to me, "Kev, I am so glad to have you and your dad up here!" Whew, finally, we uninvited guests relaxed. Dad and I were as close to heaven as you can get in Oakland, California, on one hell of a cold night!

SCHOTT DOWN IN FLAMES

As I was courting the Oakland Athletics, hopeful they would establish a home in the South Bay, I began a courtship with Dayna. I met her at Santa Clara's Decathlon Club's annual party. The Decathlon Club was always first rate and the Club masseuses had literally kept me on life support when the long hours had worn me down. The music for the party was crankin' and the drinks were flowin'. I was in the middle of a conversation with Chuck Thomas, my friend and former 49er center, regarding protecting on a forward pass. That is when I saw this stone-cold fox with beautiful blue eyes give me a smile that could melt an Alaskan icecap. I casually asked her, "What do you think of the forward pass?" She smiled and we soon became a couple.

Courtesy of The Oakland Athletics

Dayna loved sports and was the perfect partner in many trips to the Oakland Coliseum to watch the A's. We were there the night the A's set the American League record of 20 straight victories when Scott Hatteberg hit a dramatic walk-off home run to break an 11-11 tie. Not only were we there, but we were caught kissing by the cameras and shown on the Coliseum big screen!

San Jose was also courting the A's at this time but Santa Clara gained the inside track. This led to a night when I felt proud that I had come of age in professional sports know-how. I had sent Oakland A's owner Steve Schott what I called a "game plan" for baseball in Santa Clara, and damn if Steve Schott's son (also named Steve), didn't deliver that same message with style to the Santa Clara City Council. At that point I truly believed the Athletics were coming to town; I had life pumped back into my stadium dreams. Then just as quickly, prospects for an Athletics stadium dwindled. Negotiations became convoluted when *Mandalay* entered in. The press reported that talks were with Mandalay Bay Casino; in fact, the A's were dealing with Mandalay Entertainment Group! Soon it was clear that negotiations between the A's and Santa Clara were off.

September 25, 2001

(Via email from Paul Schaeffer of Mandalay Entertainment Group)

Thank You for your letter. Santa Clara appears to be quite an interesting spot for the A's. As you are aware, Peter and I no longer have an arrangement with Mr. Schott regarding the A's. Although we would reconsider the situation, that opportunity is exclusively in the hands of Mr. Schott and Mr. Hoffman. Feel free to contact me if there are any new developments.

I was impressed in my brief interactions via phone and email with both Mandalay Entertainment Group officials, Peter Guber, CEO and Co-Founder (who produced the movies Rain Man, The Color Purple, and Batman to name a few) and Paul Schaeffer, COO. These two talented individuals I would welcome to any ownership group, I was attempting to attract; however, it was not meant to be. Years later I became excited when I heard the news that Peter and Paul had purchased the Golden State Warriors along with majority owner Joe Lacob. GO WARRIORS!

I learned much from my interactions with Steve Schott and his executives, especially A's President Michael Crowley and Vice President David Alioto. This knowledge gained would be invaluable to the Santa Clara Stadium Association and future efforts to land the Niners. We also now had a completed financial analysis by PricewaterhouseCoopers and a parking study that would also come in handy years later in our attempt to move the 49ers to Santa Clara.

The constraints Steve Schott's put on the A's should be applauded for bringing back winning baseball. Those constraints as applied and practiced by his General Manager Billy Beane became the basis for *Moneyball*. It's a shame the deal with the A's didn't work out, I thought that the Santa Clara Athletics would look great across a major-league jersey.

It was hard to hide my disappointment that the A's were not building a Major League Baseball ballpark in Santa Clara and that my dream of watching a major league game with my dad in our hometown had died. However, years later Steve Schott did build a ballpark in Santa Clara. He donated a considerable sum of money to construct a new ball park for his (and my) alma mater, Santa Clara University. The Santa Clara Bronco's baseball team would be playing right across the street from where I watched them play at Buck Shaw Stadium so many years ago. This would also allow my good friend Jerry Smith, Santa Clara Women's Head Soccer Coach and a NCAA Coach of the Year, to use Buck Shaw Stadium as a new soccer-only stadium. Go Santa Clara, Go Bronco's!

HUNGRY LIKE THE WOLFF

Several years down the road, Steve Schott brought in Lew Wolff as a partner; then in 2005 Lew Wolff bought the Oakland Athletics. Upon their purchase of the franchise, Lew the managing partner, expressed an interest in building a new ballpark for *his* Athletics and the South Bay once again had great appeal. A meeting was set with a famous trio of former City leaders–Gary Gillmor, Don Von Raesfeld, Gary Hansen and myself. Lew was a man on the go and flew in on his private plane, so we met him at the Jet Center at the San Jose Airport. Gary Gillmor was upfront, "Lew, we are all getting old, so let's cut the shit and tell us straight up, do you have serious interest in moving the Athletics to Santa Clara?" Lew expounded the prospects that Santa Clara offered and I believed we were again in the hunt. I even traveled to LA to meet with Lew. I enjoyed

our talks as Lew had a great sense of humor and had me laughing often.

In my conversations with Lew, he picked up on the fact that my dad was a big Oakland A's fan and before that a booster of the Oakland Oaks, the Old Pacific Coast team that preceded the A's. I shared with Lew that my father's birthday was coming up and I asked him if it was possible that my dad might throw out the ceremonial first pitch for his birthday. What enhanced the proposition was that my father was a World War II veteran. Lew graciously arranged it, to honor my dad. Three days prior to his 83rd birthday on July 28, 2008, my dad threw out the ceremonial first pitch. Lew had the stadium announcer recognize my dad for his service as a Marine and particularly his action in the taking of Iwo Jima; and saluted him by playing the Marine anthem as he left the field. This most memorable occasion was attended by numerous members of the Moore clan.

For me, the moment turned out to be the highlight of the A's effort. Despite several more exploratory meetings with Lew Wolff, the timing, the politics, never aligned. The interest and energies of both parties dissipated. Some hope of bringing the A's to San Jose still lingers, but for me and Santa Clara, a new horizon appeared before us, and now I had a new *goal post* to run toward.

MURPHY'S LAW: IF ANYTHING CAN GO WRONG, IT WILL

To replay what followed that very special Oakland A's game….. I was discreetly talking with both the A's and the San Jose Earthquakes about relocating their franchises to Santa Clara. I was also fully engaged in outreach to the San Francisco 49ers while pursuing my Master's Degree at Santa Clara University. It was becoming quite a balancing act.

Then, I came home one night to find my wife suffering from an excruciating headache and a temperature of 104.3 degrees that wouldn't let go. I rushed her to the emergency room at the nearby hospital, where the medical staff immediately began performing test after test.

I was trembling inside, yet made every attempt to look outwardly cool and composed for my wife. My pursuit of a professional sports team coming to my town was put on hold. Priority number one was to make sure my true companion was going to be okay. Thank God, the most important test (which was heart-related) revealed that her heart was strong, and fortunately, so was her heart for our marriage.

I will not let you be tested beyond what you can endure….Corinthians 10:13

ELVIS IS ALIVE IN SANTA CLARA

During the time the Athletics were exploring the option of coming to Santa Clara, 1998 to be exact, I attended a Halloween Party at Santa Clara Councilman, Rod Diridon Jr.'s home. Of course it was a costume party and I dressed as Luke Skywalker. The party was raging when this guy showed up, decked out and bejeweled like frickin' Elvis Presley. No doubt it was a terrific Elvis costume, but it would make you laugh to see it. Right off he greeted me in the middle of the room and shouted out to the crowd: "Hey, Kevin Moore is gonna bring a stadium to Santa Clara."

Everybody laughed.

Jennifer and Michael "ELVIS" VanEvery

Elvis challenged me: "Kev, you wanna bet on your idea? I'll bet you a beer."

Because there were women there, and I was single at the time and in possession of a male ego, I raised the ante: "Let's make it a six-pack."

Elvis raised the bet, "How about a case?"

"No," said I, "might as well go for a keg."

Then Elvis one upped me: "How 'bout a TV?"

I said, "Make it a big screen TV."

In March 2014, with Levi's Stadium towering on the horizon of Santa Clara, Michael Van Every delivered on his bet, a big screen TV for the Moore household. "Kevin Moore is a special person who is large for this community. This big-mouth fan of Elvis is paid up."

San Jose Mercury News, Sal Pizarro

Yes indeed, the San Francisco 49ers *were* coming to Santa Clara–fait accompli. One might surmise this happening was twenty-eight years in the making. Yet my personal journey to this point, while long, memorable, and educational amounted to but half of the pursuit game. The steeper journey to reach the dream commenced with the second half.

"Do or do not. There is no try."–Yoda,
Star Wars Episode V-The Empire Strikes Back

Photo Courtesy of The San Francisco 49ers

HALFTIME DREAM SEQUENCE: 49ERS LOCKER ROOM

My mind is obsessed over a Santa Clara home for the 49ers. One night in a deep sleep I see myself in the 49ers locker room in dialogue with Coach Jim Harbaugh. He's dressed in his black sweatshirt, khaki pants, a black SF cap on his head. The dream was clairvoyant; I could see in the future the value of a professional sports team in my hometown. Coach Harbaugh was plumbing my philosophy of sports and motives for bringing the team to the Mission City.

Coach Harbaugh: Kev, you're fighting the good fight. You've been in the ring for some time without a knockout punch. Must be discouraging. How do you look back on those failed attempts to land a sports team?

Kev: You have to pay some reverence for those failed attempts. In whatever the heck you're struggling with, those failures can set up a good foundation for your future efforts. I recollect some philosopher said, "The greatest success comes from failure."

Coach: Like the Nelson Mandela quote: "Difficulty breaks some men but makes others." So give yourself a high five. But tell me, Kev, what's your motive for bringing the 49ers to Santa Clara?

Kev: Now imagine this: Los Angeles doesn't have an NFL team, but little Santa Clara can host the 49ers! Think what that does for community pride when you go to a stadium we made happen. I love my little town. Santa Clara is an underdog and its fun when the small guy beats the big guy; it's the Rocky Balboa story.

Coach: "Yo, Adrian" – I love it. Sounds biblical, like David and Goliath. Is there some tie-in with religion?

Kev: Yes, for me everything is linked to prayer. I'm always praying Hail Marys. Praying to Jesus is great, but if you pray through the intercession of his Mother, it's even better. So I pray a lot of Hail Marys.

Coach: Can you throw in a couple Hail Marys for the team, Kev?

Kev: Yes, every game, coach!

Coach: So bringing a stadium to Santa Clara is in a sense doing God's work?

Kev: Yes, it's been a journey of faith, but also a journey of timing. I remember your predecessor the great Bill Walsh would say, "Like a boxer, you need to beat your opponent to the punch." That's what we're doing to get the 49ers to Santa Clara.

Coach: But why a football stadium of all things?

Kev: It relates to that euphoric feeling I had the first time I walked into Buck Shaw Stadium as a five-year-old. The game is a celebration of life and it doesn't matter if you're black, white, green, red or disabled; everyone seems to be ONE when you're rooting for your team.

Coach: Well, if you believe you can make us a new stadium in little Santa Clara, I am confident the entire 49er family will attack this endeavor with enthusiasm unknown to mankind.

Kev: Say, Coach, I've got a question for you: "Who's got it better than us?"

Coach: Nobody!

Coach Harbaugh walks off into the mist, pumping his arm high in the air.

"Afford each person the same respect, support and fair treatment you would expect if your roles were reversed. Deal with people individually, not as objects who are part of a herd–that's the critical factor."

- Bill Walsh, San Francisco 49ers, Hall of Fame Head Coach

Photo by, Michael Fallon, courtesy of 49ers Museum presented by Sony

3rd
Quarter

A BILLION TO ONE

1997, living in the Islands, from my Diamond Head Road address, I mailed a letter to Mr. Carmen Policy, President of the San Francisco 49ers, suggesting moving the team to the City of Santa Clara… NO RESPONSE.

1999, back home in Santa Clara, I wrote a letter to Mr. Larry Thrailkill, Team President of the San Francisco 49ers, suggesting a move to Santa Clara… NO RESPONSE.

2003, I persisted in writing another letter "To Owner Dr. John York"... NO RESPONSE.

2004, I hand-delivered via a training complex security guard a letter to the 49ers Corporate Office directed to Dr. John York, Owner, San Francisco 49ers. The note was re-directed to Larry MacNeil, Chief Financial Officer… RESPONSE!!!

Across my series of letters I sought the advice of the old guard. These former Santa Clara City Council members had led the city through various policy changes and numerous development projects. Now, while many seekers of information or advice visit the library, read books, or go online, my modus operandi was to pick up the phone and call somebody or to sit down with someone. I had a lot of conversations with former City Manager Don Von Raesfeld (25 years' experience), and former Mayors Eddie Souza and Gary Gillmor. Gary was also my boss in real estate. One day early on I went to Gary and said, "I'd like to see if we can bring the 49ers here. What do you think the odds are for bringing the 49ers to Santa Clara?" Gary opined, "Well, knowing what I know from growing up in San Francisco, your odds are a billion to one." As weeks progressed and letters of interest passed, I went to Gary again, "Well, what are the odds now?" "We're probably about a million to one now." Then we got to 50 to 1; then we were even money!

Stadium Talks That Started With a 2003 Letter, Built on Decades of City Work.
By Carolyn Schuk–SANTA CLARA VALLEY WEEKLY

The infrastructure that brought Levi's Stadium to Santa Clara was in place because of city planning starting back in the late 1960s, with one of the great partnerships in city history - former Mayor Gary Gillmor and former City Manager Don Von Raesfeld.

A YORK IN THE ROAD

Back at the Training Facility and Corporate Headquarters, when I approached him out of nowhere, the security guard was amicable. "Friend," I said, "I have an important letter for Dr. John York."

"Pertaining to what?" he asked.

"Pertaining to Santa Clara's interest in building a new stadium for the team," I replied.

"Then you need to talk to Larry MacNeil. I'll see to it that he gets this letter, he works here on site."

"Thank you."

Sometime thereafter, I was planning to visit in-laws in Roseville near Sacramento when I got a phone call from San Francisco 49ers Chief Financial Officer Larry MacNeil inviting me to meet with him. "I'd love to meet in person with you, how's this next Monday?" I suggested.

"Can you meet with me tomorrow?" he retorted.

Finally I had my chance to inform a Niners executive why their new stadium should be in Santa Clara. So Larry was digging at me trying to uncover who I am, what credibility I have, what information I can offer. He played devil's advocate to much of my reasoning. I was doing my best fighting for Santa Clara. At some point I saw an opening, an angle that might appeal personally to him as well as to other Niners' personnel who spend their days here at the corporate office or training facility. "Larry, wouldn't you rather build a new stadium right outside this window?" as I swept my hand toward an expanse of prime real estate. "Aren't you tired of the frequent commutes back and forth to San Francisco?"

Larry nodded yes, and said, "but we still have to convince the Yorks."

Such a meeting was set with Dr. John York, Owner. The City of Santa Clara met him with a delegation of the old guard, council members and community leaders. Our gathering took place at team headquarters, 4949

Confidential

December 19, 2003

Dr. John York
San Francisco 49ers
4949 Centennial Boulevard
Santa Clara, California, 95054

Dear Mr. York,

There is an excellent opportunity to build a world-class San Francisco 49ers' Stadium less than ¼ mile from your franchise headquarters in the City of Santa Clara.

My name is Kevin Moore. I am a lifelong resident of the City of Santa Clara and I successfully founded the Santa Clara Youth Soccer Park adjacent to your 49ers headquarters and the San Tomas Aquino/Saratoga Streamside Trail, between Centennial Boulevard and Paramount's Great America Theme Park.

As an executive board member of the Santa Clara Stadium Association, I successfully led the Santa Clara City Council to open stadium negotiations with the Oakland A's last year. The Price WaterhouseCoopers financial analysis we completed for the A's discussions demonstrates significant potential for a stadium in Santa Clara. Additionally, I strongly believe the current Council would welcome the San Francisco 49ers to the city.

There are many advantages to locating the new 49ers Stadium in the City of Santa Clara.

Due to the Santa Clara Convention Center and Paramount's Great America Amusement Park, site access is unparalleled to any other location in the Bay Area. Two major freeways serve this entertainment area. Great America Parkway has been widened to handle major events. Light Rail and Amtrak both serve the area with existing stops.

And, Santa Clara, with Intel, Sun Microsystems, Applied Materials, etc., continues to be the Bay Area's high tech center.

Unlike other potential Bay Area stadium sites, Santa Clara's location has infrastructure in place, and is ready for construction.

I look forward to the opportunity to discuss with you in confidence the many benefits of locating your new San Francisco 49ers Stadium in Santa Clara.

Best regards,

Kevin Moore
P.O. Box 286
Santa Clara, CA 95052

Centennial Boulevard, now renamed Marie P. DeBartolo Way. There was trepidation on our part as York came to town; we were conscious of educating him on our capabilities without leading him down a delusive path. John York had assumed control of the franchise following the team's incredible feats under Eddie DeBartolo. He dealt with salary cap issues and San Francisco's protracted talks of a new stadium. The team had abysmal seasons in 2004 and 2005. Media and fans cast John York in an unfavorable light.

I knew the York family was Catholic; I could identify, having had 19 years of Catholic school education. I knew that John and his son Jed were alumni and supporters of Notre Dame University; I grew up watching and loving Notre Dame football. Alas, I understood there was no love lost between the family and San Francisco Mayor Gavin Newsom; I was now in competition with Gavin to be the home for the 49ers. Dr. York and I traded Catholic school stories, anecdotes on playing and coaching basketball, shared similar religious school experiences, and critiqued the shortcomings of the San Francisco site.

John York was very cordial in talks with our delegation. The outcome was that both parties got to know each other over the course of six weeks. We provided ownership information critical to stadium construction, the likes of which they could not have received from San Francisco in a timely manner. As additional details were needed, our Assistant City Manager gathered data together and drove over to 49ers offices with due haste; this impressed the 49ers brass.

ALL ROADS FROM CANDLESTICK LEAD TO THE MISSION CITY

The Niners were overdue vacating Candlestick Park for a modern stadium. The 1960 structure suffered damage from the Loma Prieta Quake of '89 before the start of the third game of the Bay Bridge World Series. The Giants left in 2001; the 49ers were eager to follow. The Stick was deteriorating year by year, and safety was becoming as big an issue as amenities for players. San Francisco hoped to retain the Niners in a redevelopment plan, a combined stadium and shopping/entertainment mall at Hunters Point. The

City secured federal financing to clean up toxic pollution at the former Naval Shipyard–how appealing was that! And while the City was set for a new ballot measure, what the City could not guarantee was a definitive source for the $500 million in roads and bridges needed for a new stadium. Hence, the plan never moved forward nor did funding for infrastructure, notably roadways for traffic. For fans entering and exiting The Stick, the traffic backups were miserable.

For the Niners to compete in the NFL, the team needed a new stadium as soon as possible. Santa Clara was one of the few places that had critical infrastructure in place. The Santa Clara site was well situated, centrally located in the heart of Silicon Valley. Infrastructure was in place thanks to the foresight of Santa Clara's past political leadership. Their designs enabled a big industrial base generating revenue for city services. The city was a model for how to plan right. Great America Parkway and Tasman Drive, key access roads, feed off two freeways, 101 and 237. Caltrain and Southern Pacific pass alongside, as does VTA Light Rail. San Tomas Aquino Creek Trail (which I had a hand in creating) leads right to the stadium for walkers and cyclist.

Prescient city planning and development of the Great America Parkway was crucial for north Santa Clara whether for industrial development or a stadium. Neither the City alone nor the State could meet the funding need at the time, so in the early 1970s City Mayor Gary Gillmor and City Manager Don Von Raesfeld met with Governor Ronald Reagan to cut a deal. Santa Clara lent the State money needed to build the Great America interchange and within the decade the State paid it back in full. That infrastructure was key to the listening ears of the Niners. Someone before me was looking into the future literally paving the way for the land lease agreement for the 49ers training facility, stepping stone to a stadium. The old guard created a strong offensive line posed for a professional sports complex.

BARE ASS AND BOLD ASS POLITICS

I tried to bring a national sports franchise to Santa Clara by working from the outside. As I watched politicians who screwed up one stadium deal after another, I knew I had to be on the inside. The Santa Clara City Council had split on matters dealing with stadium issues where a single vote could have made the difference. I was certain I could influence others in a positive way to support a stadium. Not to diminish other equally important matters that I wanted to affect, it became apparent, I *had* to run for office to get in the game.

A first step to become a Council candidate was to "pass an audition"–an endorsement interview for one's candidacy. The interview was in the County Building in San Jose. I dressed in a pair of khaki pants, wore topsiders and a West Valley-Mission College Trustee polo shirt. When I arrived in the office area, not a soul was around. I sat down in the waiting area for my appointment with the Endorsement Interview Committee, then "the Irishman" walked in. I've known him for many years, he's always been cordial but he hung with a different crowd than I did. The Irishman said to me, "Kevin, you look real yuppie dressed for your endorsement, right? Here, let me show you your chances of getting this endorsement." He turned 'round, pulled down his pants and bare-assed me. "These are your odds of getting an endorsement," he said, and he walked into the main room. (For the record, a short while later, I called him on his behavior and said his act was on videotape. It was not, but he could not be sure. I had him over a barrel, bare ass and all, and eventually gained favor with the Irishman because of it.)

The interview room was a hostile environment. One question concerned my involvement in a political campaign about a mayoral candidate who opposed Patty Mahan, a person I fully supported. This other candidate had acted in a manner I found questionable. While I would credit him with hard work as a councilman, in my opinion he was a factor in the failure of the Oakland A's negotiations. He could not be trusted with the Niners. I would relate my perception of this fellow to a '60s theatrical hit, *How to Succeed in Business without Really Trying*. The song *Gotta Stop That Guy… before he stops me* became my theme song.

The incident in question related to a full-page ad I had taken out to advise Santa Clara citizens of questionable practices by this candidate. The press wrote scathingly about my ad. Committee members were shocked by the action and put the screws to me, but I didn't cave. They asked, "In hindsight, would you take such action again?"

I told them absolutely, yes, I'd do it again. I knew my honest response would be respected and believed it would work in my favor.

MEANWHILE … BACK TO THE BURNING BUSH

I threw the BMW into reverse and extricated myself from the bush outside the 49ers corporate office. As I escaped further embarrassment and distanced myself from the scene of the mishap, I started to chuckle over what had happened. The slip-up paled in comparison to my conviction; I believed I was called to lead a 49ers exodus from Candlestick to the promised land of Santa Clara. I applied all that I had learned and avoided errors that plagued earlier efforts. I promoted Santa Clara well. This freak accident should not have jeopardized that effort. I trusted we were in the game. Nonetheless, the 49ers' announcement was out of my hands. Only a higher power would know how this would emerge. I was hopeful that the 49ers would not renege on Santa Clara.

As I drove carefully away from Niners headquarters my emotions started to soar. My mind recalled the old classic song, *A Nightingale Sang in Berkeley Square,* by Bobby Darin. The song expressed exactly what I was feeling. Bobby Darin gradually elevated the emotional level. How the music and lyrics scaled up was brilliant. When the listener thought the song had reached its high point, Bobby brought the emotion still higher. So it was with me, pure elation escalating from each note struck with the Niners. And when Darin sings, *that heart of mine, it beats loud and fast like a merry-go-round in a fair*–that's exactly what I felt–my heart beating loud and fast like a merry-go-round in a fair rising up and down. Leaving the 49ers headquarters that evening I really hoped I was on the road to my dream.

When the Lord saw that he turned aside to see, God called to him out of the bush… Exodus 3:3

BETTING AGAIN ON THE NINERS

Later that night I attended an event in downtown San Jose. The local major league soccer team was changing its name from the *Clash* to the *Earthquakes*. The press was there, notably Sports Columnist Mark Purdy of the *San Jose Mercury News*, along with media from San Francisco. Seemingly out the blue, but assuredly in front of the out-of-town press and notably Raj Mathai of NBC, Mark Purdy asked, "Hey, Kev, where do you think the 49ers will end up?"

I was feeling optimistic that tomorrow's announcement would come down for us. So I said, "I think they'll come to Santa Clara." Everybody laughed at me. But I trusted my gut feeling and bet Purdy a beer. I told the San Francisco crowd that I'd bet them too. Sure enough, the next day the announcement hit the airwaves: The San Francisco 49ers were focused on Santa Clara as their future home. Purdy phoned me up: "You already knew, didn't you? You knew the Niners were to formally announce their interest in Santa Clara."

I laughed, "Yeah, so I did, and you owe me a beer, my friend."

THE LITTLE CITY THAT COULD

Obviously the 49ers' announcement stirred the press and more and more were following and investigating the story. Santa Clara had occasionally referred to itself as the *Can-Do City* and so the Mercury News sent out a reporter to ascertain if it was really possible for a little city like Santa Clara to accommodate a fabled NFL franchise like the 49ers. The reporter challenged me: "Santa Clara is such a small town, do you really think you can pull it off? Seriously, Kevin, how can a little town like Santa Clara support a professional sports team the likes of the 49ers? You're not Chicago, LA, or New York."

I quickly decided not to engage her in a debate, but rather I said to the reporter: "If you're an investigator, then go into City Hall and find out what Santa Clara owns."

So the reporter made tracks and later responded to me: "Wow, all I can say is 'wow,' you guys own more land outside of your city than inside City proper. You own a billion dollar infrastructure with extended city lands under redevelopment..."

To which I added, "And we have our own utility plant right outside the future stadium walls" (an asset that later shone bright on the fact that the lights went down in Candlestick Park during a Monday Night Football game).

NOVEMBER 2006. John York, in a news conference in Santa Clara, CA, declares that while the San Francisco 49ers are still listening to San Francisco, we are shifting our focus to Santa Clara.

SANTA CLARA "THE MISSION CITY"

In 1796 Jose Francisco Ortega, scouting for the Portola-Serra party, became the first European to visit the fertile valley that later became known as the Santa Clara Valley. The Franciscan padres selected this fertile valley to establish the eighth mission, Mission Santa Clara, named for Saint Clare. The mission was founded January 12, 1777.

In 1836 control of Mission Santa Clara was taken from the padres and turned over to civil commissioners. By the 1840's the American frontier had expanded to California and new settlers began arriving in the area. When promises of great wealth failed to materialize during the Gold Rush of 1849, many of the gold seekers turned to the *gold* that was the fertile land of the Santa Clara Valley and began to settle in Santa Clara. Santa Clara incorporated as a town on July 5, 1852, and became a state chartered city in 1862.

Santa Clara is located 42 miles south of San Francisco and at the center of Silicon Valley. In 2010, population within the 18 square miles city limits was 118,830 persons. The city is home to Santa Clara University and headquarters for several leading technology corporations.

Of further interest is this August 2, 1990 article by David A. Sylvester, Chronicle South Bay Bureau, titled: *The Santa Clara Story–How the Giants Would Fit In.* ... To excerpt:

Santa Clara is located 42 miles south of San Francisco. That was a one-day horseback ride between the two outposts when a mission was founded there in 1777. The San Francisco mission had been established a year earlier.

The namesake is St. Clare de Assisi, a 12th century nun who was inspired to live a life of poverty and prayer by St. Francis. St. Clare founded the Poor Clare Sisters. In the custom of the Spanish Catholics, the city took St. Clare's name to receive her blessing and protection. This blessing would include the Giants. "This doesn't mean they'll win every time," said the portress at the Poor Clare Monastery in Los Altos Hills.

Let us pray the blessing now extends to the 49ers!

Photo by W. J. Parolini

49ers launch public effort for Santa Clara stadium

WARM RECEPTION FOR TEAM: COUNCIL MEETING DRAWS FANS

QUESTIONS STILL UNANSWERED: SIZE, FORM OF CITY'S INVESTMENT

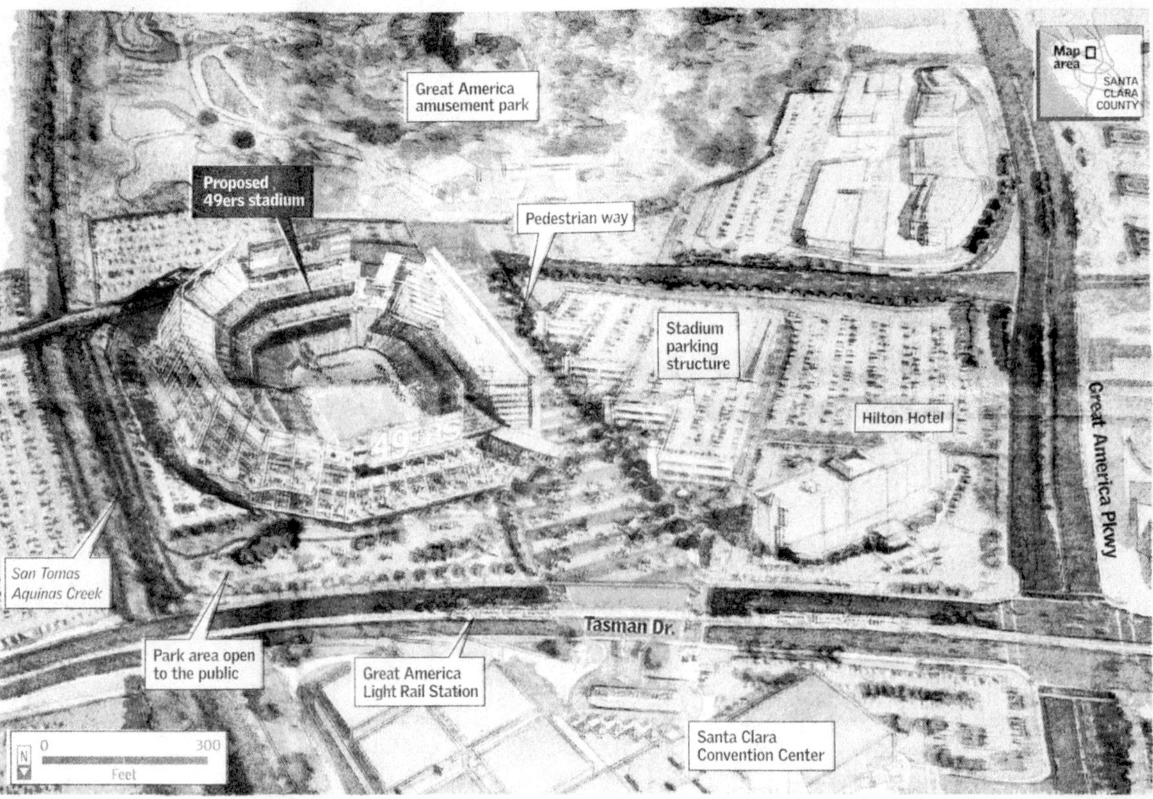

Source: Illustration provided by San Francisco 49ers

MERCURY NEWS

VENUE, SLATED FOR 2012 SEASON, COULD COST UP TO $800 MILLION

By Mike Swift and David Pollak
Mercury News

In the first public step on what could be a 5½-year journey to build an NFL stadium in the South Bay, Santa Clara's city council opened public discussion with the San Francisco 49ers, city residents and dozens of the team's fans Tuesday night.

More than 100 people, including several former 49ers players, crowded into a public hearing that was more about raising questions than answering them. But team officials told the gathering what council members already knew: A stadium site in a parking lot next to Great America is the 49ers' first choice for a new home by the 2012 season.

"It's very simple," said Jed York, son of the 49ers owners. "In Santa Clara, everything seems to add up," including access to public transit, a vibrant business community, shopping and other amenities — and, York added, "a community that seems to know how to get things done."

Most in the overflow crowd appeared to welcome the idea for a South Bay stadium. The Santa Clara chapter of the team's booster club, in fact, canceled its own meeting so members could attend.

"It'd be wonderful to have

See **49ERS**, *Page 6B*

NHAT V. MEYER — MERCURY NEWS

San Francisco 49ers fan Jan Boehm of Sunnyvale shows off her jersey Tuesday to team executives shortly before they made their first public pitch for a Santa Clara stadium.

SANTA CLARA–RIGHT PLACE, WRONG TIME

Since 1989 I've pursued the dream to bring a major league sports team to my city, Santa Clara, CA. To many it seemed like Kevin Moore's pipe dream. Yes, it was a personal mission but the idea made practical sense. Santa Clara is not only a part of the San Francisco Bay Area, but it is central to Silicon Valley. And while it would have been my delight to secure the San Francisco Giants or the Oakland Athletics, the Giants were off the table with a new ballpark. The Athletics seemed to be in limbo between staying in Oakland or relocating to San Jose, except that the Giants and Major League Baseball were not willing to give the A's territorial rights needed to build in the South Bay. If such a move made sense to the Giants and Athletics, why not a 49ers stadium in the South Bay? And what better city than *little* Santa Clara?

So now, the 49ers were at our doorstep–it was time for me personally to step up. I made the overture, paved the approach, argued to convince politicians, real estate developers, and the public that *we can do this*. Now, if I could only convince my wife!

Julee and I had met in December 2003. She was gorgeous and smart, and she loved baseball. Julee had quickly won my heart. I willingly abandoned dating and threw myself wholeheartedly into this relationship. I, who always recommended dating a person for several years before "tying the knot" picked out an engagement ring after only a couple of months. We married on October 17, 2004, the anniversary of the earthquake that interrupted the Bay Bridge World Series at Candlestick Park.

In early years, because of my pursuit of a sports team for Santa Clara and because of the dot-com bust, we struggled with our finances, and with serious health issues.

But now the dream and the journey were REAL. It was my dream, my mission, my reputation, and *our* future on the line! And this fortuitous happening could not have come at a more unfortunate time. Life rarely follows our timetable and we often find ourselves in predicaments not all of our own making, though it's been established that inviting the Niners to Santa Clara was foremost my doing. But at this time, my wife and I were suffering through several trials and tribulations beyond what sports campaigning might foment again. Santa Clara was assuredly the right place for the 49ers, but for me personally "it was the best of times, it was the worst of times."

I FEEL YOUR PAIN ... NO YOU DON'T

So now the real challenge had begun–constructing and implementing a Strategic Plan for securing the 49ers with a new stadium in Santa Clara. On the homefront construction was underway at the Moore house. I had checked us into a very average hotel on the El Camino Real. At 2:45am tooth pain hit me and hit me sharp! I've had broken bones before, taken elbows to the jaw, endured many other pains, but this combination of a dry socket and root canal was like nothing I ever suffered through. The only thing nearing temporary relief was keeping the gum area ice cold, which I achieved through multiple trips to the ice machine down the hall. After hours of raiding the ice machine I called my dentist in the wee hours of the morning. Thank God he was at his patient's beck and call. He agreed to see me in his office. My wife drove me down and his assistant rushed me into to the dentist chair. First question, "Would you like Novocaine?"

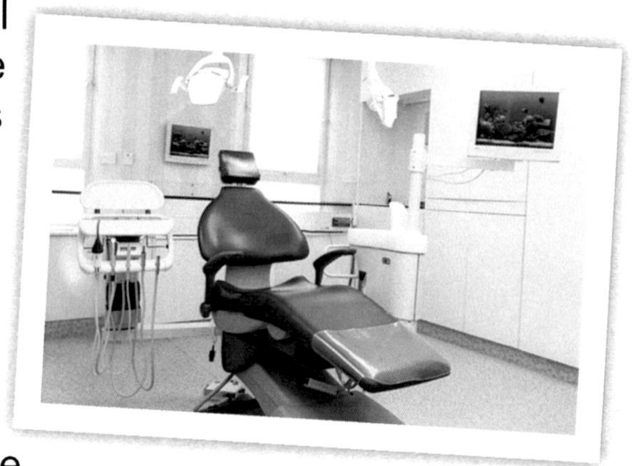

"Uh huh," I barely mumbled. Then he shot me up with Novocaine for good measure, but surprisingly it had little effect. We waited and tried again to no effect until finally a third try achieved the intended results. At that very moment the assistant rushed in and exclaimed, "Your wife is hunched over and calling for you!" I staggered half-looped out of the dentist chair to reach the lobby and witnessed my wife crumbled up in severe pain. I looked up at the staff and they understood–I needed to get her to the hospital immediately.

In the emergency ward doctors determined that my wife needed to undergo appendicitis surgery. Nervous, worrying in the waiting room, I was relieved to hear the doctor's first words upon his exiting the operating room: "The surgery went well." An hour later I was able to see her in the recovery room and was thankful to see her beautiful eyes open. But my relief was short lived. F--, F--, F--, the Novocaine just wore off!

Back to the hotel and again I beat a path to the ice machine. Then for a change of scenery I made a break to Jack-in-the-Box on El Camino Real and affirmed that a large vanilla milkshake helped relieve the pain for some 20 minutes. Half an hour later, I was back at Jack's on Stevens Creek Boulevard scoring a chocolate shake. Not wanting either to arouse suspicion that I'm casing any one joint or to look conspicuously crazed, I hit another Jack-in-the-Box for a strawberry shake–scoring the Neapolitan hat trick! Bloated with milkshakes I made my way to an all-night Walgreens, where I pleaded with the pharmacist to provide me something to medicate my pain. Returning to the hotel, I couldn't resist one more vanilla milkshake night cap. Obviously, my interactions with the Niners' organization took a backseat to other life priorities at the time.

"Behind every beautiful thing, there's some kind of pain"– Bob Dylan, Musician

THE COMMISH IS COMING TO TOWN

With 49er interest in Santa Clara now serious, Larry MacNeil informed me that the NFL Commissioner, Roger Goodell was coming to town to survey the landscape. He had an hour layover to assess the city as a possible-stadium site. We were thrown into a panic over what to show him. Niners staff were already making plans to take him to Santa Clara University, Intel Corporation, and other various places. "No frickin' way," I said to MacNeil, "we won't have time to do all that. Here's an idea, let's take him to Great America amusement park for a ride on the Sky Tower and give him a view of the whole valley." But then I quickly realized the park was closed and we'd have to get it open. We got hold of the parks general manager, who himself seemed extremely enthused about hosting the NFL Commissioner, "Yeah, no problem, we'll do it."

Now we had to buy a gift. The Commissioner of Football was coming to town and it is customary to present a distinguished visitor with a welcoming gift. I drove over to City Hall but the staff had nothing of the sort, not even a paperweight or City pen set. Staff suggested the Chamber of Commerce so I hurried there only to have the Chamber give me a bag of miscellaneous crap, coupons to various tourist sites, and the like. We were not going to hand him a bag of miscellaneous trivia, no way man, that wasn't going to happen on my watch.

My money situation was tight at the time but I was determined to purchase something special. I sped over to Santa Clara University and searched through the bookstore, where I found a stylish golf jacket with the logo of the Mission and the name *Santa Clara*. I figured the Commish likely played golf and would appreciate this gift more than crappy coupons, miscellaneous stickers and visitor maps. Now to get the gift wrapped.

My mom, now retired, had managed Macy's Gift Wrap department for twenty-five years and is the world's best gift wrapper. I took her the Santa Clara Mission golf jacket and asked, "Mom, can you give this an A-1 gift wrap, you know, like really over do it?" In her supply closet Mom found sparkling gold wrapping paper and a roll of wide red ribbon; she wrapped the present so beautifully in 49ers' colors.

The Commissioner's limousines followed our lead to the amusement park where the general manager was awaiting us. As Roger Goodell stepped out of his limo I handed him the stunningly wrapped box. He was surprised to say the least, and expressed his genuine appreciation at this goodwill gesture.

Next we took the ride up to the top of the rotating Sky Tower overlooking Santa Clara Valley. Our host strategy was for Mayor Patty Mahan to escort and engage the Commissioner and leave me to talk with his other executives. Patty enthralled the Commissioner, pointing out various Valley assets: freeways, trains, light-rail, hotels, Silicon Valley industries–everything that made Santa Clara a premium site. I hung back chatting to the other executives, one of whom was legendary NFL officer Joe Browne, with whom I hit it off immediately. The showcasing of Santa Clara from the Great America Sky Towers couldn't be topped. Someone reported that he overheard the Commissioner comment, "Well, this all makes sense, this is a no-brainer."

SMILE, YOU'RE ON CANDID CAMERAS

The *Santa Clara Focus* announcement from John York, President of the San Francisco 49ers, launched within hours a flood of media calls. One call came from Channel 7 News, which wanted to interview me and Mayor Patty Mahan. In turn, I called Patty and told her the News wanted interviews. I would pick her up and we'd drive together to the Santa Clara Convention Center. In my front seat sat Mayor Patty with this movie-star-worthy makeup

Photo by Ray Rodriguez, Jr.

kit, similar to what my sister Reenie toted when she danced on Broadway. She pulled out cosmetics and accessories, prepping as I drove, finishing as I hung a right turn prior to the Convention Center, bypassing Channel 7.

"I thought we were going to the Convention Center?" Patty asked. "You just passed the entrance."

"Yeah, I know, we're going to go by 49ers headquarters first. And be prepared, you're going to give more interviews in the next 48 hours than you've done in your entire life."

We turned into 4949 Centennial Boulevard and the media was swarming in front of the 49ers Headquarters, blocking the entrance. Parking in front of the commotion of trucks, lights, reporters and cameramen, I suggested that Patty sit tight a minute while I go have some fun. I stepped out of the car and headed toward the line of news vans. On the side of the first van I saw *Channel 2 News*. I went up to the van and asked, "Hey, is this Channel 7 News?"

The crew replied, "No, this is Channel 2." I was professionally dressed to the hilt in my suit and tie, all Gucci'd out. As I headed past, the reporter asked, "What are you here for?"

I replied, "The Mayor has an interview with Channel 7."

The news reporter fires back, "Can we get an interview with her?"

"I'll ask her," I said, stalling as I approached the next van, Channel 5 News. "Hey, is this Channel 7 News?"

"No, this is Channel 5."

"Okay, sorry," and started walking on.

Its reporter similarly asked, "What do you want with Channel 7, are you here for the news story?"

"Yes, Santa Clara's Mayor has an interview with Channel 7 and Channel 2."

"Well, how about her interviewing with Channel 5 as well, can we do that?"

"I'll have to ask her and get back to you." And so it continued right on down the line of news teams. I reported to Patty that four stations now wanted interviews. We reminded ourselves of our agreement not to do battle with San Francisco. We would stay positive, not be presumptuous, but speak to the potential that Santa Clara offered as a new stadium site.

"Okay, let's roll," said our Mayor exhaling. She got out of the car with a Hollywood glow ready to dance on Broadway. She nailed the first interview and was into the second when a cameraman and reporter looking desperate, shouted, "Hey, you're Vice Mayor Kevin Moore, correct? Can you step in here and get in the picture?"

"The Mayor will be right with you," I deferred.

"Please, we'd like to get you into the picture now. Raj Mathai is in our studio and we are LIVE. We want a live interview with you, please over here." The first question was something like: Senator Diane Feinstein is upset that Santa Clara is making such a push for the Niners when the focus should be on the team remaining in San Francisco. What's your comment on this?

"I have nothing but good things to say about Diane Feinstein. I'm a big fan of hers and she's helped us with our utilities and that's one reason that Santa Clara is a good site for a stadium." The cameraman perceived the cleverness and smiled. Then came the shot across the bow. "Gavin Newsom is equally perturbed at your bold and eager overtures wanting the team in Santa Clara when the San Francisco 49ers ought to reside in the city of their namesake. Your comments to Mayor Newsom?"

"Hey, I love San Francisco. I've got nothing bad to say about San Francisco or Gavin Newsom. But you do know that when it came time for him to choose a college, he chose Santa Clara University, so he knows how good our city is." The cameraman laughed so hard he almost dropped his camera.

As had I, Patty avoided the pitfall of taking on San Francisco, speaking candidly on three news networks for the promise that Santa Clara offered: "For those from San Francisco who (see) this decision as an intercity rivalry... we do not see it that way. This site would provide Bay Area fans a great game day experience."

SHUTTLE DIPLOMACY – WHO'S ON FIRST

I now became engaged in what one of the 49ers political consultants called "Shuttle Diplomacy." I was largely directing the negotiations, which City Manager Jennifer Sparacino, graciously and surprisingly was allowing me to handle. In such delicate dealings and maybe in part due to my ADD, I preferred face-to-face meetings as opposed to talking on the phone. My shuttle diplomacy developed a cadence:

THE PLAYBOOK
THE SAN FRANCISCO 49ERS
OF
SANTA CLARA

"The art of fighting, without fighting!"
-BRUCE LEE

(*Revised: 4/15/2008, 8/31/2009, 12/14/2009)

I drive to the 49ers headquarters at their training facility in north Santa Clara to report that "the City can do this, and this, and this."

"No, no, no" the 49ers would say, "We can't do that, that or that. But we can do this, this, and this."

So I'd get back in the car, drive down to City Hall and report, "Well, the 49ers can do this, this and this, and they can give us that and that."

To which the City Manager would say, "Well, okay, we can do this and this, but we can't do that."

So, I'd drive back to the 49ers and state, "Well, we can do this and this and this, but the City won't do that unless you do this."

And the Niners would counter, "Well, we can't do that, unless you do this."

And when they did say they would do this, I had to ask, "Okay, are you sure you can do this?"

They'd answer, "Oh absolutely we can do this if the City can do this and this and this, and as a matter of fact, you don't even have to do this, if you do that."

And I would drive back again to City Hall and translate to the City Manager, "They can do this, this and this, can't do that; but if we do this, they will do this; but they're never gonna do that, unless we do this."

She'd come back, "Well, I can do this, but you're going to have to see if they can do this and this." And so I'd drive back over there and repeat the whole process again and again and again. It was a never ending merry-go-round. Mayor Mahan's description of the process: It was like courting, and we were on our first date.

"Kevin Moore was the catalyst that brought the 49ers and a receptive city council together..."

Miles Barber, Publisher, Santa Clara Valley Weekly Newspaper

R-E-S-P-E-C-T ... FIND OUT WHAT IT MEANS TO ME

San Francisco Chronicle writer John Coté invited me to meet with him for an interview barely a month after the Forty-Niners' decision to build a stadium in Santa Clara became official. John drove down from San Francisco to meet at the Hyatt adjacent to the stadium site. We sat in the hotel's Asian restaurant. The day was unusually hot for December and apparently caught the Hyatt's climate control system off-guard–their air conditioning was off. So when the waitress asked if we would we like something to drink, I ordered a beer. John looked slightly surprised. "I don't usually drink during an interview, but hey, it's hot in here." John was a very congenial fellow who sincerely wanted to hear my story involving the 49ers negotiations and those earlier Giants and Athletics campaigns that set the stage for this current effort.

John had done his homework and was forthright. He brought up what mayoral candidate "Big Mac" had said--that I can't be trusted. Ironically, that was more or less my news ad claim against him. I confided that we were mutually opposed, to say the least. I suggested to John that he look on the Fair Political Action Commission website, where it shows Big Mac was fined.

The rest of the interview was upbeat. John did a wonderful job of going beyond the obvious to uncover my lifelong passion for sports in my hometown. His feature article raised stock in my credibility and promoted my dream to a front page news story.

DECEMBER 18, 2006. San Francisco Chronicle front page.
Profile / Kevin Moore by John Coté Chronicle Staff Writer

Santa Clara dreamer nears goal line. Vice mayor is finally close to bringing city a pro sports franchise.

"When Kevin Moore talks sports, any sport, hang on for the ride. The Santa Clara vice mayor, a driving force behind the effort to bring the San Francisco 49ers and their stadium to the South Bay, talks mostly in streaming narratives. That's especially the case when the discussion turns to youth soccer, baseball, or college basketball."

Under a photo of me standing on bare ground with arm extended and hand balancing a football, The *San Francisco Chronicle* affixed the caption: "Kevin Moore hopes this site in a parking lot by Great America will be home to the 49ers new stadium."

SAN FRANCISCO HITCHES HOPES ON HETCH HETCHY

The City of San Francisco was desperate to retain the team. Without a stadium proposal to go forward, their primary tactic seemed to be to prevent any Santa Clara deal. Someone, somehow, learned that the San Francisco Public Utilities Commission owns a pipe that supposedly lies under part of the land where the Niners hoped to build its stadium. The pipe is part of the Hetch-Hetchy system, which carries water from the Sierra Nevada snowmelt to the San Francisco Bay Area.

Lisa Lang, 49ers vice president, said the stadium footprint does not interfere with the Hetch Hetchy: "We're well aware of the right-of-way and the fact is that the Hetch Hetchy runs along the fence at Great America and does not interfere with plans to build."

At the same time San Francisco was attempting to halt negotiations in Santa Clara, they had to watch their posture so as not to raise the ire of Niners management. "Publicly, San Francisco officials are going out of their way not to antagonize the team. We are not focused on the situation surrounding the Santa Clara site at all," said a spokesman for Mayor Gavin Newsom. "We have a strong working relationship with Dr. York and believe we've got a great plan for San Francisco, and that is all we are focused on."–Oh, really?--Not!

One official speaking anonymously because of the sensitive nature of the issue called the pipeline revelation "unbelievable leverage for us. It's quite remarkable." Reporter Robert Handa called me and met me at the site and helped to clear up the misinformation San Francisco was feeding through other news sources.

JANUARY 2007. Feasibility Study. The City Council adopts guiding principles and the process for a feasibility study of the proposed stadium, including a schedule of public meetings.

JUNE 2007. SiliconValley Central. "New Study on Stadium Shows $650 Million in Regional Economic Benefit"

DECEMBER 2007. City Manager Jennifer Sparacino says the city's general fund should get a bigger direct financial return. Sparacino's staff prepares to issue its final recommendation on the project.

JANUARY 2008. Negotiations Begin. The feasibility study is complete, including economic benefits, public safety impacts and financial options. The City enters into non-binding negotiations with the 49ers.

OH GREAT, AMERICA, TAKE US ON A ROLLER COASTER RIDE

Cedar Fair Corporation, owners of California's Great America, were not pleased with the likelihood of a 49ers stadium next door. Great America was not the first nor the only NIMBY "Not In My Back Yard" opposition we would encounter.

Perhaps Santa Clara misread Great America. We thought the Park would be receptive if not welcoming to the prospect, working with us for mutual benefit. Wrong. Cedar Fair had an executive named Duffield E."Duff" Milkie (honest to God) and he started derailing the City's efforts with the Niners. We sent people to talk through agreements, but Cedar Fair became locked on wanting an enormous buyout. This action shocked the 49ers' Larry MacNeil. We wondered if those "carnies" were crazy?

Prior to this, the Park had petitioned the City to build a wooden roller coaster. My thought, if you're not gonna play ball with us, then we're not gonna play ball with you. The City was very aware that nearby building occupants already had sound complaints with the rides. The response to Cedar

Fair was to simply deny their petition to construct the wooden roller coaster. But compromise came when Richard L. Kinzel, President & CEO, wrote to the City of Santa Clara:

> "Cedar Fair must protect Great America and our substantial investment in that park and we will do that. Cedar Fair will also devote the time and resources necessary to thoroughly pursue good faith negotiations with the City and the 49ers in an attempt to resolve the difficulties presented by the stadium proposal in an attempt to avoid the need for a more formal defense of our legal rights. . . On behalf of Cedar Fair and California's Great America, I would like to underscore my commitment to the City of Santa Clara and to the community."

Meanwhile, a backup deal was brewing to sell the Park to a company that owned part of Ghirardelli Plaza in San Francisco, investors thinking they'd buy it to help the Niners. The Niners were also willing to put up speculative money. In the end Cedar Fair did not sell, perhaps seeing advantages to nearby development. After years of going up and down, round and round, the "carnies" were pacified. Then I said to Great America, "You know what? You guys need to get a wooden roller coaster in there."

TURF WAR

S.F. back in running a day after Niners walked away . . .

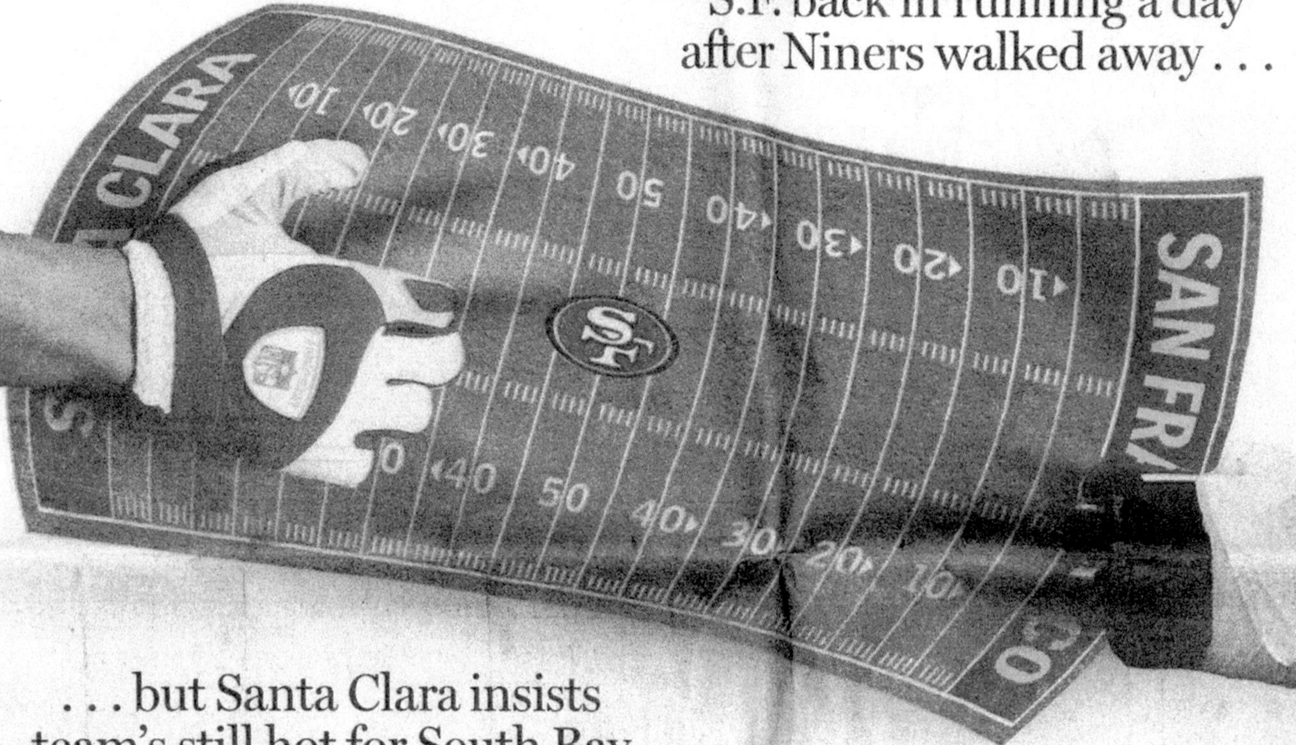

. . . but Santa Clara insists team's still hot for South Bay

PAI — MERCURY NEWS PHOTO ILLUSTRATION

COURTESY PATRICIA MAHAN

Santa Clara Mayor Patricia Mahan says the city remains the Niners' top choice for building a football stadium, despite the team renewing talks with San Francisco.

By Mary Anne Ostrom
Mercury News

Talks are back on between the city of San Francisco and the 49ers. Sort of.

One day after team owner John York dropped the bombshell that he had cut off negotiations with the city and planned a move to Santa Clara, a temporary truce was brokered by Sen. Dianne Feinstein, D-Calif.

But York made it clear Friday that he also would continue talks with Santa Clara. Mayor Patricia Mahan said York left her a voicemail message Friday making it clear "we are still the top choice."

Whether a real tug-of-war will emerge over the 49ers remains to be seen, but many people in both cities are shaking their heads remembering long, bitter fights of past decades for baseball's San Francisco Giants and Oakland A's.

"This is a powerful sense of *déjà vu*. San Francisco is a tough nut to crack. You can't roll over them like most owners can in other cities," said Rich DeLeon, a retired San Francisco State University political science professor who wrote about the San Francisco Giants' on-again, off-again threats to move to the South Bay and elsewhere.

And some in Santa Clara are wary, too.

See **TURF WAR**, *Page 17A*

JUSTIN SULLIVAN — GETTY IMAGES

San Francisco Mayor Gavin Newsom said he didn't believe the Niners' move to Santa Clara was a "fait accompli," and that the city is reviewing its options for keeping the team in town.

SANTA CLARA COUNCIL ROSTER

Patricia Mahan

As Mayor through 2010, Patty led the charge for the Niners. Personally and politically, she wanted the team for Santa Clara. She charmed the NFL Commissioner Roger Goodell with her polish and acumen to a height of 500 feet on the Sky Tower ride. She was the perfect tour guide to show the Commish the benefits of Santa Clara's infrastructure. Patty was excellent in her commercials supporting the stadium. An attorney by profession, she understood negotiations.

Jamie Matthews

Jamie was first a City Council member then Mayor down the back stretch of our efforts to bring the 49ers to Santa Clara. Jamie was valuable in making pro-stadium commercials, building consensus among council members, walking precincts, and planting campaign lawn signs, sometimes into the wee hours of the night.

Lisa Gillmor

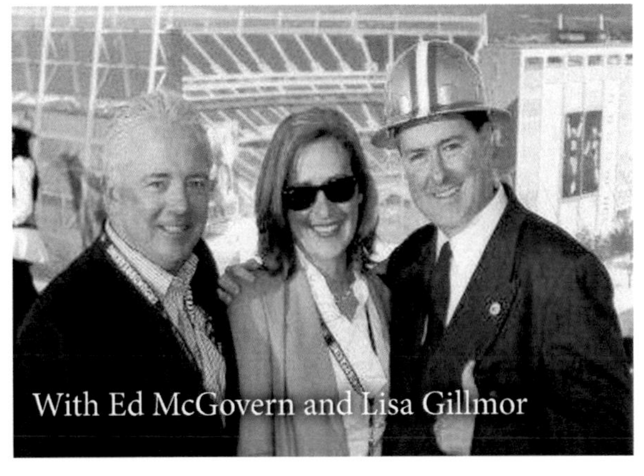

With Ed McGovern and Lisa Gillmor

Lisa has been a friend and associate for many years. She and her father have served the Council well. I would always pester her to help on the 49ers effort. She thought I was crazy chasing this dream. I'd walk into her office and before I could utter a word she'd say, "Okay, Kev, the Niners are coming to Santa Clara, I get it. Now get out of here." But in time, she too was bitten by the bug and was outstanding and fearless in working for the cause. As a former council member her service with the stadium booster group was invaluable. She can kick butt to make things happen. She returned to the Council and helped invigorate and steady the process after the Stadium election. She's always been one very smart, very savvy business person and faithfully cares about the City of Santa Clara.

Pat Kolstad

The best proof of Pat's position appeared in an exchange we had in the early stage of interfacing with the Niners. Pat came up to me before a council meeting and said, "Moore, that's the stupidest idea I've ever heard."

"What is?" I asked.

"Trying to bring the 49ers to Santa Clara." A week later in the same spot he cornered me to say, "Hey, Moore, we've got to make this happen."

"Make what happen?" I feigned knowing.

"The stadium," he exclaimed.

"Well, I was standing here last week and somebody who looked just like you said that would never work."

"Well, I changed my mind."

Pat excelled in large group presentations, defending against stadium opponents.

Joe Kornder

Joe was a former Santa Clara high school teacher, administrator and one-time basketball coach, now councilman. Despite concerns about the deal, he delivered some critical votes and was credited with garnering funds from the 49ers to cover extra security measures for the stadium.

Dominic Caserta

Dom favored a stadium deal from the beginning and consistently contributed his support to the measures necessary to advance the initiative. Dom was featured in a pro-stadium commercial.

Will Kennedy

We had worked well together mutually supporting our election to council. Will resembled *Harry Potter* and so we called him by that nickname. He adamantly opposed the stadium deal. Will was a protection law-

Santa Clara's Mayor, Four Past Mayors and 17 Current and Former Members of the City Council

Patricia Mahan
Mayor

Larry Marsalli
Former Mayor

Larry Fargher
Former Mayor

Eddie Souza
Former Mayor

Jamie Matthews
City Council Member

Dominic Caserta
Vice Mayor

Gary Gillmor
Former Mayor

Joe Kornder
City Council Member

Kevin Moore
City Council Member

Lisa Gillmor
Former City Council Member

Gary Hansen
Former Vice Mayor

Pat Kolstad
Former City Council Member

Aldyth Parle
Former City Council Member

Dave Tobkin
Former City Council Member

Don Von Raesfeld
Former City Council Member
and City Manager

Steve Lodge
Santa Clara Police Chief

yer and could find any argument to oppose stadium measures. He feared that the stadium would change our town, but I think he overlooked the economic benefits and his projections missed the mark. I like Will and his family even though they were Minnesota Viking fans.

Jamie McLeod

Jamie's arguments kept changing from time to time. We were cordial and actually had some good laughs. She's a Green Bay Packers fan. I told her flatly, "You're on the wrong side of the tracks; and oh, the Niners are going to beat the Packers this week." And, of course, they did.

Debi Davis

Debi was elected to the City Council in 2012. As chair of the Marketing Committee, she has taken a leadership role in upscale economic development around Levi's Stadium, such as the proposed Joe Montana Entertainment Complex.

Jerry Marsalli

A strong stadium supporter whose knowledge from decades of being a member of the Santa Clara Police Department helped in the process of opening the stadium. He is the son of former Mayor Larry Marsalli, whose support on our stadium effort was valuable.

Teresa O'Neill

Teresa has done a good job making sure the City's and the 49ers' committment to the Santa Clara voters are fulfilled.

Jennifer Sparacino

The City Manager was small in stature, a former school teacher who some called the Iron Butterfly. When I became a councilman, she was good to me. We held a lot of private meetings. I never took her on in public, but there came a point where she seemed bent on killing the deal. It was so big, so overwhelming. And then Jennifer suddenly, sadly, lost her husband in the thick of it all. Her ambivalence was influencing council members and staff. I went to her one day and said, "Go kill the deal."

She gave me a look that asked, What do you mean?

I said, "Just go kill the deal. Your people are putting out stuff that's not helping us." I think at that point the deal was coming around and she rose to the occasion and supported it, managed it, and performed admirably in negotiations.

Julio Fuentes

Julio became City Manager in 2012 and has wisely promoted the stadium to bring substantial economic development and fiscal stability to Santa Clara.

Ron Garrett

When we first met in his Assistant City Manager's office there was one stadium file on his desk. Next thing you know there were hundreds of 49er stadium files engulfing his entire office. It was funny to see the rapid development of his priorities. Ron was a nice guy who took marching orders from his boss. He hung with it and helped drive the negotiations with the Niners.

Ren Nosky

Ren was a City Attorney who worked overtime through various legal issues, which helped advance the final Niners agreement.

Jerry Keyser

As Chairman of the Board of Keyser Marston, Jerry assisted the City of Santa Clara in determining the feasibility of the 49ers deal. His solid expertise in real estate and development helped us make sound decisions on several major related areas.

David Hatheway

David was first-rate in representing the City of Santa Clara in managing the stadium project.

STADIUM IN SOUTH BAY

HOW SANTA CLARA LANDED THE 49ERS

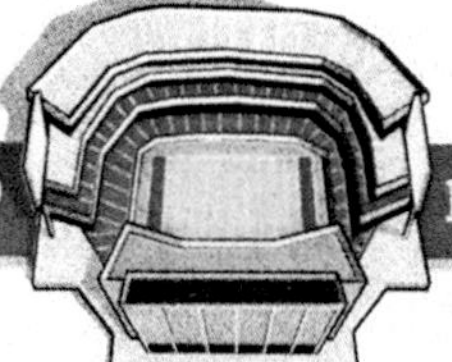

MARK PURDY'S LINEUP | ELEVEN STADIUM POWER PLAYERS

WIDE RECEIVER
Jennifer Sparacino
City Manager, Santa Clara
City's lead negotiator with 49ers; built and signed off on a package economists call one of the most favorable stadium deals for a city in the modern era.

RUNNING BACK
Patricia Mahan
Former Mayor, Santa Clara
Grabbed the ball and ran with it, even taking NFL commissioner Roger Goodell up the revolving tower ride at Great America to convince him of the site's potential.

QUARTERBACK
Jed York
Owner and CEO, 49ers
Beginning in 2007 as director of strategic planning through promotion to CEO, York drove the project and made all the key decisions until a deal was done.

FULLBACK
Kevin Moore
Councilman, Santa Clara
Made the city's initial contact with 49ers, cleared a political path through the city flow chart to turn the concept into a reality.

WIDE RECEIVER
Jamie Matthews
Mayor, Santa Clara
Took office after the election, and as a stadium booster has successfully guided the stadium authority through various hoops to make sure nothing went sideways.

RIGHT TACKLE
Jim Harbaugh
Coach, 49ers
As the stadium timeline reached a key stage -- where suite and ticket seat licenses needed to be sold to make bankers happy – Harbaugh led the team to the NFC title game and renewed fan enthusiasm.

RIGHT GUARD
Gavin Newsom
Former Mayor, San Francisco
Pulled his city out of the running and opened the door to Santa Clara because he kept pushing the 49ers to a Hunters Point location they didn't want.

CENTER
John York
Owner, 49ers
Jed's father, after making the initial bold call to end talks with San Francisco and shift the focus to Santa Clara, snapped the ball to Jed while continuing to serve as an adviser.

LEFT GUARD
Larry MacNeil
Chief Financial Officer, 49ers
Did the heavy lifting during negotiations and played a pivotal role in crafting compromises and terms acceptable to both sides.

LEFT TACKLE
Ed McGovern
Political and Election Consultant
A veteran and savvy warrior on the Bay Area political landscape, he played a major role in assembling the successful Santa Clara stadium election.

TIGHT END
Goldman Sachs, Bank of America, U.S. Bank
Collectively backed stadium with up to $950 million in loans.

PAI/BAY AREA NEWS GROUP

SAN FRANCISCO ROSTER

John & Denise York

John was very personable and easy to talk with. However, that is not how some of the Bay Area sports media and fans saw him. His wife, Denise, sister of Eddie DeBartolo, first stepped in when Eddie stepped down. Eddie's success in leading the Niners was a hard act to follow. John and I didn't have many conversations but those we had were pleasant. He is a retired cancer research pathologist who was successful in the medical field. Their decision to pick Santa Clara for the site of the stadium was bold. His announcement of focusing on Santa Clara took courage and he pulled the announcement off with flying colors.

Jed York

When Jed was given the reigns of the 49ers, his leadership provided a huge boost. Having managed in a Fortune 500 company, Jed took over as 49ers President with experience and skill. He's also very charming. I could be myself and talk uncensored around Jed. In meetings at headquarters he'd work his way in to say hello and lend a positive presence. Jed was certainly the right guy at the right time, and without him this shared vision would not have become a reality. Jed, along with his dad, John, spent many days and nights in Santa Clarans' homes assuring residents of the good the 49ers would bring to the community. I am utterly amazed how Jed with his busy schedule always found the time to answer my phone call even during meetings with the NFL.

Gideon Yu

Apart from executive duties with the 49ers, Gideon was a financial officer for Facebook, YouTube and Yahoo. He was the quintessential stadium financing guru. No Gideon, no financing. Gideon is a good friend. He's been off the executive grid, though he's still a co-owner of the team.

49ers Co-Owner Gideon Yu

Larry MacNeil

Larry was the 49ers CFO and was the point person for the stadium.In his office was a picture of young Larry in an argyle sweater at a ski resort, looking just like Greg of *The Brady Bunch*. I was comfortable around him. I'd talk to Larry four or five times a day. He kept the line moving. However, Larry sometimes was the bearer of bad news if there were points of difference. Throughout the campaign Larry listened, then acted. He was invaluable. We would strategize together often and were almost always successful in our efforts.

Lisa Lang

Lisa was the face of 49ers community and public relations. She was great, she got it, she walked the extra mile. There was a kind of synchronicity to her business acumen. Even when my ideas seemed crazy, she trusted me and I trusted her and she delivered. I was selfishly sad to see her leave the organization because I enjoyed working with her as she was so supportive. We worked together quite a bit on shaping the message for the campaign and determining what would be shared with the media. There is so much more to Lisa and her many good deeds.

Andy Dolich

Andy is flat-out brilliant. He` joined the 49ers in 2007 as the Club's Chief Operating Officer responsible for day-to-day business operations. Andy was a former executive vice president of the Oakland Athletics where he increased season ticket sales and attendance. Andy's advice was critical.

Gregory Carey

Greg was Managing Director of Goldman Sachs Investment Banking Division and managed the financing of Levi's Stadium. The savings on long-term interest payments for the Stadium Authority were estimated at $100 million because of the financing arrangements. Greg's professionalism and humor were refreshing when processing through piles of information and over hours of meetings.

Harry O' Brien

Harry was the Niners' Attorney, always on his A-game in detailing stadium contracts and legal aspects. Harry knows when to gather information and when to talk. You could almost hear his brain ticking; he was often steps ahead of others in the room.

Patty English

Patty was a 49ers Vice-President and extremely intelligent, a class act. She was a ray of positive energy throughout many important meetings.

Ed McGovern

The top political consultant for the 49ers was a savy political strategist and most influential and dedicated consultant, rarely taking a breath to relax. Ed was keen on building public consensus and support, and coordinated extremely well with both the City's leadership and the Citizens for Measure J committee. Ed was credited with the idea of having John and Jed York personally visit residents in their homes.

Rich Robinson

Aside from being a 49ers fan, Rich reached out to help the campaign. He was valuable in gaining the support of former City Council members who had opposed previous stadium efforts.

Jude Barry

Jude was a consultant hired for his excellent relationship with the press. He helped land a first-rate endorsement editorial from the *Mercury News*.

John Wasson

John was one of a handful of acknowledged experts in the design and construction of sports stadiums.

Jack Hill

Jack was Project Executive brought in from Texas to manage various stadium projects. His passion was evident and infectious.

Gary Filizetti

In initial meetings with the Niners I pushed hard for them to hire Gary to work on the project. They were only committed to hiring one firm and they really liked Turner Construction out of Georgia. I knew the stadium opposition would complain if we hired a construction company out of state. I was ecstatic when Gary's company, Devcon, Inc. and Turner Construction were both hired. When opposition complained about an out-of-town construction company, I asked Gary during a Council meeting where he went to high school and college. Gary resounded "Santa Clara High School and Santa Clara University." You could have heard a nail drop as the opposition was hammered backwards. Local boy makes good!

Gavin Newsom

The former Mayor of San Francisco (and Santa Clara University Alumnus) was known for his striking stature and looks. Gavin was lambasted for an affair with his campaign manager/best friend's wife – which some believe may have been an advantage for Santa Clara. Gavin became a perfect villain for Niners management. Without a viable plan, Gavin could do little more than raise objections to Santa Clara. At a point he was rallying to save the team, but by then the deal was pregnant. Gavin ran for Governor and lost. Then later he ran for Lieutenant Governor and the night he celebrated his election, Santa Clarans were celebrating the Stadium vote. Postscript: I ran into Gavin at the Paul McCartney Farewell to Candlestick Concert. He shook my hand and congratulated me: "Good job." I thought that was a class-act gesture.

"The main ingredient of stardom is the rest of the team."
– John Wooden, Legendary Basketball Coach

Photo credit: Br. Thomas C Bracco S.J.

January 10, 2008

Dear Mayor & Council Members,

"On behalf of the San Jose Sports Authority, San Jose's Sports Commission, we applaud your efforts to move forward on a stadium that will serve Santa Clara, Silicon Valley, and our region.

"The Santa Clara Chamber of Commerce and the San Jose/Silicon Valley Chamber of Commerce join together to support the feasibility of a new stadium for the 49ers football team in the City of Santa Clara.

"Silicon Valley Leadership Group believes that while many matters remain to be resolved, from transportation and parking plans to final building costs, the team has laid out a very solid package that we support. Team owner John York has pledged to four principles regarding the stadium:

1. Significant team contribution (about 42.6% from team & NFL).
2. No new taxes on residents or businesses in Santa Clara
3. No negative net impact on Santa Clara's general fund
4. If cash reserves from Silicon Valley Power are used, it should not impact ratepayers.

JANUARY 15, 2008. After a year of extensive research, discussions, public comment, and an eight month feasibility study, the City Council determined that the proposed stadium presents potential …

THE PERIOD 2008-2009. EIR Analysis - A comprehensive Environmental Impact Report is prepared by an independent consulting firm including analytical reports on land use, geology, hydrology, visual resources, biological resources, hazards and hazardous materials, cultural resources, transportation and circulation, air quality, noise, utilities and public services. The Draft EIR receives extensive public review and comment before the final EIR is accepted by the City Council.

TO BBQ OR NOT TO BBQ...THAT IS THE QUESTION?

A closed-door session is not public; suffice to say that a critical vote of the Council necessitated a meeting. I arrived at the meeting early and anxious knowing every such vote could become crucial. More than just a quorum, every council member should have been in attendance. Jamie Matthews, as a stadium advocate, had a key vote. When I looked around the table, Matthews wasn't there. I was nervous that decisions would be adverse to the campaign. Not leaving the vote to chance, I phoned Jamie as the meeting was called to order. "Hey, Jamie, where are you?" He told me he was flipping burgers over at Santa Clara High School.

"What?"

He explained that he was flipping burgers at a BBQ at the school's special event. I expressed shock and desperation and a little exaggeration, "Unbelievable! We're having one of the biggest votes in the history of the City and you're flipping burgers?" A long pause followed.

I said, "Hey, brother, I love you man, and I'm not going to get mad at you here, I'm just going to always remember that when we had one of the biggest votes in the history of the City and the stadium, you were flipping burgers over at the high school. Remember that."

He responded that the City Manager told him that it was not an important meeting, and that he needed to grill some more burgers.

Jaime Matthews Volunteering

I concluded, "Well, hey, I hope you grill some great burgers while the stadium deal gets burned by the opposing council members sitting across from me." Some fifteen minutes later Jamie shows up wearing a big red BBQ apron and smelling like smoked charcoal. His vote and support that evening was crucial. We passed an important measure, one more critical step in a long climb. I will always remember him in his BBQ outfit and that he showed up for this important vote.

SOMETHING'S GOTTA GIVE–HER OR ME?

The City Attorney saved the deal and then, to put it bluntly, was more or less forced to resign. After a string of meetings between the 49ers and the City, Niners executives were not able to move the ball down the field and were ready to punt. Their offense encountered a stiff defense in the City Manager; they questioned whether she was trying to run out the clock and end the game. In a critical sidebar, Lisa Gillmor, longtime Santa Clara business woman and community leader, not on the council at the time, persuaded the City Attorney to go rogue and meet with the Niners. So the City Attorney, Lisa, and I, met with the Niners on our own. The Attorney's analysis, her recommendations, and moreover, her positivity saved the day and kept the deal alive.

Now the discord between the City Manager and City Attorney became tense. The City Manager wanted her out, but the Attorney would not roll over, and the City Manager was use to getting her way. The Attorney, though tough-minded on all legal matters, was always willing to offer advice and think strategically. She did what she believed was right for the City. But the disagreement reached a point where it was to be one or the other. The City Manager wielded a lot of power, while the Attorney had her detractors. When it came to a head, an agreement was worked out for the Attorney to step down. I truly regretted it had come to that, and to this day I give the Attorney credit for her gumption. This was another critical action on the part of an individual who thought and acted to disrupt the bureaucratic system for a greater good. The 49ers stadium might not be here today if it were not for that rogue meeting. This unnamed Attorney and Lisa Gillmor are unsung heroes of the stadium project.

STRIPTEASE FOR A VOTE

As a City Councilman on the go, given the demands of negotiating with the 49ers organization via shuttle diplomacy–maintaining my health was essential. I generally stayed healthy, hitting the sidelines no more than a day or two a year. But wouldn't you know… a closed-door session was to be held after the public council meeting to review items privately. Yet another crucial decision would be made in this intricately woven tapestry of reports, agreements, logistics, financing, and procedures. And I came down with the flu! I had a fever that set fire to my body. The room was hot, and becoming even hotter with the heated discussion. I was flush, beads of sweat ran down my face and onto my shirt and even trickled on to my paperwork. The council's bickering was driving me out of my frickin' mind. But I could not leave the debate. I'm thinking practically out loud, "Come on, make a frickin' decision; I've got to get the f-- out of here."

A male council member almost always wore a spiffy suit and tie, while the ladies dressed in pantsuits or dresses. I could no longer tolerate the fire burning inside. So I took off my jacket and hung it on a coat hanger behind me. This council member was talking on and on before another started rambling on and on and I thought to myself "F--" and I loosened my tie. I was sweating even more and still the chatter continued. I removed the noose from around my neck and draped the tie over the jacket. The meeting dragged on. Another jerk (I'm negative to all at this point) didn't know what the f-- he was talking about but was expounding ad infinitum about God knows what. I was uttering expletives under my breath as I unbuttoned my dress shirt starting at the top button and working down, unbuttoning one after another.

Now my shirt was wide open across my chest with shirttails hanging down the sides of my seat. "F-- it." I stripped off my dress shirt and threw it across my tie and jacket hanging behind me. Now I was down to my soaked white Hanes undershirt and ready to frickin' kill somebody. So I leaned forward into the discussion and exclaimed, "Look at me, I'm sick! I'm sitting here in my drenched t-shirt right now and I want to let you know that things could get pretty ugly pretty soon. We've got to vote *now,* because if we don't, this t-shirt is coming off."

A colleague of mine reacting swiftly pleaded, "Let's call for a vote." We voted and I was out of there in ten seconds flat.

NOT A PENNY MOORE!–S.O.S. ON THE 101 FREEWAY

Niners management was often just a phone call away when City staff were at loggerheads on various matters involving the stadium. In one such meeting the City Manager informed the Council that the Niners settled on an amount of money for security and that her staff was comfortable with the agreement. An unnamed council member went crazy; similar actions had earned him "the Crypt Keeper" moniker. He protested that the City needed more money for the cops. Well, holy shit, the Niners had just granted a record amount of money. But the Crypt Keeper would not relent. If the 49ers CFO were present he'd have thought "forget that guy!" But this well-intentioned individual refused to budge. So I suggested to the City Manager: "Why don't we call the 49ers and tell them we need more money for security." I said this even as I knew MacNeil had adamantly expressed that the only way Santa Clara was getting any more money out of the Niners was over his dead body, but we had to break this logjam.

I repeated, "Why don't we take a recess and have the Assistant City Manager call the 49ers?" Another council member agreed. The Mayor called a recess and the Assistant City Manager went to make the call. As others loitered in the hallway I ducked into the mayor's office and called Larry MacNeil to give him the heads-up that the Assistant City Manager was going to call him. He was driving on the 101 freeway to San Francisco. I told him I was here with the mayor and the former mayor, then took a deep breath and began, "Remember, how you said that you'd wouldn't give a penny more for security?"

"Yeah," he responded. "Well, we need more money"

There was a pregnant pause. I was counting on the fact that he didn't want to see the deal fall apart. He exclaimed, "I'm on the freeway, let me pull over." He pulled over and asked me to explain what led to the call, and I did carefully, avoiding anything discussed in closed session. In the ensuing follow-up conversation with the Assistant City Manager, he conceded additional funds. The deal was getting closer.

THE FLYING NUN GROUNDS THE UNION

My father was a union man, a bricklayer by trade. The union made sure that workers' rights, wages, and working conditions were maintained. The union was very good to our family.

I remember one special Christmas. My dad had never been busier working overtime, double overtime on weekends, and had received hazard pay for the construction of a brick furnace. Dad said to me, "Kev, write down your Christmas list, write down everything you want. This is the one and probably only year that you're going to get everything on your list!" That Christmas was unbelievable, thanks to the dedicated union working dad.

The unions were good to me as well. I've always had union support when I ran for office. That said, the union could be demanding in the interests of its members. This was the case with the stadium deal related to services and then to construction. At meetings early in the process the union was represented by an officer I referred to as "Union Boss." I found the Union Boss rather pushy, yet because of my positive history with unions I hoped these negotiations would be successful. But the Union Boss was not satisfied; he wore on my positive feelings. Already we had held two volatile meetings; I was to the point where I wanted to choke the guy. He equally pissed off our mayor and former mayor.

At a third meeting, union members were at the table with Niners–and when I say *at the table,* I mean it literally. We were seated around this big, long, wooden conference table with the "SF" logo in the center. I had heard that Eddie DeBartolo had this conference table specially built for executive meetings. As the talking bore down, it was my perception that the Union Boss was basically telling the Niners, "If you don't hire the Union, you're going to have trouble getting the stadium built." I was ready to jump out of my skin. As I looked around the room, I could see that I wasn't alone. The Niners' executives sat stone-faced. I wondered how far they would let the Union Boss push them before they would just call the meeting to a close and go look somewhere else to build their stadium. It seemed the Union Boss wasn't listening to a word they said. And soon their silence only amped him up more. Couldn't he read their body language?

More and more the Union Boss was sounding like Al Pacino in *The Godfather gambino-ing* the Niners. His presentation was going over like a lead balloon. I feared there would be a war of words with the *familigias* and it wouldn't be pleasant. If this went on much longer, my dream would become a nightmare; I was getting extremely uncomfortable.

Now, I was seated in the cheap seats at the far side of this long table and I had to come up with some diversion. I looked intently at the Union Boss, trying to both divert his stammering and attract his attention. As I stared at him he reminded me of this old actor from a '60s TV series. I raised my hand; he nodded toward me. The thought spilled out of my mouth, one of the more bizarre things I've ever said in an executive meeting. Looking back it was either a stroke of genius or a gift from God. I declared, "You know who you look like?" Every head in the room turned toward me. You could have heard a pin drop. He paused.

I said "Do you remember *The Flying Nun*?" You remember that TV show? Well you look like Sister Bertrille's friend, the guy she hung out with, Carlos Ramirez, played by Alejandro Rey." Most everybody nodded, then exploded with laughter–the remark was so far-sided, so off the wall.

The Union Boss looked like I'd just thrown a pie in his face. He didn't pick up on my game plan to distract him, probably he was thinking I was some kind of a smart-ass. From that moment on his presentation fell apart. He was unable to pick up the thread of what he was saying before my colorful interruption.

Maybe it caused him to reconsider his position. The stadium would be a boon for the union and its membership. The Niners had already bent over backwards to accommodate the union. The Union Boss' tone softened and the parties were able to resolve the conflict. Thank God for *The Flying Nun*.

"It goes over like a Lead Zeppelin"–Sister Bertrille, The Flying Nun

OPPOSITION ROSTER

"YOU MUST CONFRONT THE DARK SIDE"

To be sure, there were people opposed to Measure J, an Advisory Vote asking Santa Clara citizens for approval to build the stadium. Campaign staff had a nickname for the opposition, the "J-Haters," because many of them oozed with hate for Measure J. Those on the opposite side of the contest were also referred to as "the Dark Side." I soon realized that the facts of the deal apparently had no bearing on what most of them thought, said, or did. Supporters who knew these leading opponents sensed that some fell in love with the camera and desperately tried to stretch their fifteen-plus minutes of fame. Personally, and as representative of the people, I tried to accept and relate to most of them before and after the stadium victory. Here were my favorite challengers with my admittedly biased impressions.

Darth J-Hater

He headed the opposition. He gleamed with excitement whenever he got the spotlight. We would have late-night pancake summits where I would try to convince him to turn away from the Dark Side. He would talk about the stadium and various ways to lay it out, but his ideas would not have worked. His favorite line at council meetings was: "None of us are paid, we are all volunteers." In the wee morning hours after the election win, on the parking lot where the stadium was now to be built, the 49ers raised a sign that read: "Future Home of the San Francisco 49ers." Both of us were there, wearing our battle scars, tossing around a football in friendliness.

The First Female Fire Chief

She stood out vividly. She was a real shit stormer, a tough opponent, the equal of Jack "Hacksaw" Reynolds on the campaign field. My disappointment in her was that she went up to San Francisco and solicited money from their people to kill a Santa Clara stadium deal. That did not go over well in Santa Clara. She claimed that the Santa Clara Fire Department was going to be badly cut after the stadium was built. Her dire predictions earned her a spot in a video with a toy fire truck and a siren blaring behind her. The skit was something that should have been on *Saturday Night Live*. I laughed a long time after seeing that video, it provided welcomed relief from the campaign drain. We made peace after the election; she actually has a great dry sense of humor when she is not chasing windmills.

Mr. Finger

He called me offering to host a debate at his house. He claimed that a number of his neighbors hadn't yet made up their minds on the issue and would like to see an honest debate. Council member Matthews and I did not trust him so we drove by his house in the middle of the night on a reconnaissance run. What we saw all over his front yard were *NO on STADIUM* signs. Months after Measure J passed, Mr. Finger got so pissed off at me at a public meeting that he flipped me off. I knew cameras were not filming the audience but I threw out a bluff to make him think his action was recorded. He freaked out and after the meeting anxiously wanted to talk with me. I told him to buzz off.

Mr. San Jose

He used to be a good drinking buddy until he demostrated that politics and friendship don't necessarily mix. I met Mr. San Jose through my sister. We used to dine together at this popular Chinese restaurant with our partners. As a lawyer he was articulate and could give every reason why the sky is falling.

The Big Mac

He was not only anti-stadium at first but, more so, *my* most outspoken critic to the press. His posted attack on me read: "He is known in some political circles as 'the stadium Energizer bunny,' because he just keeps pushing and he keeps going and going and going, trying to pawn this city land off to a sports franchise to put a stadium there. Why is Kevin Moore the lead agent trying to push some stadium there? It's not his land and it's not his money." Big Mac finally limped in with support for the Niners and did reach out to compliment our success. We made peace.

Mrs. Farmers Market

Mrs. Farmers' Market expressed her concern about the stadium's impact on the city: "I want to make sure the city and residents are not going to be tied to something that benefits the few and costs a lot of us. I don't want to be giving this away to a private company in some sweetheart deal." I've never believed in trickle-down economics, and yes, the stadium is funded in part, and most to be enjoyed, by high roller corporations and individuals. But the City Council negotiated aggressively to bring Santa Clara *the* best deal of any major sports stadium agreement. After the election Mrs. Farmers Market and I reconciled. I have to admit she was an excellent planning commisioner.

The Mouth Piece

Shown on TV walking door to door, this opposition mouthpiece claimed "J" was losing 3-1. She must have been walking in Sunnyvale.

SANTA CLARA STADIUM SCORECARD

TAKING SIDES ON PLAN FOR NEW 49ERS STADIUM

BY JULIE PATEL ■ MERCURY NEWS

There are the good guys and the bad guys. That's what newcomers to Santa Clara politics are often told. Who's who depends on your view on issues such as development, police and firefighters' rights, and now — a new stadium for the 49ers. In a city where loyalties run deep and political allies can help shape careers, you're either with the team or against it. But keeping track of the players isn't just sport in Santa Clara these days. The politics behind the stadium deal may lead to one of the South Bay's most sig-

See **STADIUM**, *Page 8B*

PAI — MERCURY NEWS

THE STADIUM BACKERS
THOSE WHO SAY 'LET'S TRY TO BUILD IT'

◄ City Councilman **Kevin Moore**, who first reached out to the team about the idea of a stadium

City Councilman **Dominic Caserta**, who wants the idea to move forward

◄ Santa Clara County Assessor **Larry Stone**, who backed efforts to bring pro sports to the South Bay for years because it's part of building a thriving metropolitan area

Former City Manager **Don Von Raesfeld**, who proposed tapping city utility reserves to invest in the stadium

◄ Former Councilwoman **Lisa Gillmor** and her father, **Gary Gillmor**, left, the city's first elected mayor, who support big-vision ideas for Santa Clara

Neil Struthers, CEO of the Santa Clara and San Benito Counties Building & Construction Trades Council, said the stadium will provide critical jobs

ON THE SIDELINES
THOSE WHO SAY IT'S HARD TO SAY

◄ Mayor **Patricia Mahan**, vice mayor **Will Kennedy** and council members **Jamie McLeod**, **Pat Kolstad** and **Joe Kornder**, who need more information

Former City Clerk **Judy Boccignone** and former Mayor **Bill Gissler**, who co-chair a group that will review the proposal's fiscal impacts

◄ City Manager **Jennifer Sparacino**, who says she and her staff will provide information about the proposal and eventually make recommendations

Former Mayor **Judy Nadler**, who was opposed to the A's deal, and doesn't plan to take a stand this time because of her role as an ethics professor

THE FISCAL WORRIERS
THOSE WHO SAY 'NOT FOR $180 MILLION'

◄ Residents such as **Bryan Patterson**, left, and **Joan Tomlinson**, who wrote city representatives to oppose the stadium because of traffic, noise and other problems

John McLemore, who opposed the A's project when he was on the council

◄ **Kate Grant**, a Santa Clara resident and executive director of a local non-profit, who said the city has bigger priorities

Former planning commissioner **Byron Fleck**: "We don't use Santa Clara residents' monies to subsidize private billionaires."

◄ Planning commissioner **Karen Hardy**: "I don't want us to wave our pompoms around and say, 'Yea, look at us. Isn't it great?' and when the band goes home, we're left with a bill to pay."

Sunnyvale resident **Mark Maloney**, who said surrounding cities will be affected by traffic and other issues

Source: Mercury News interviews

DO YOU KNOW THE WAY TO SAN JOSE?

Mr. San Jose was articulate and not afraid to speak out in large stadium meetings. He was most definitely anti-stadium.

One day when dropping by the real estate office of a friend (whose dad had served the City), my friend mentioned "Mr. San Jose is looking at buying a new house in Santa Clara."

I begged my friend, "Do the 49ers and Santa Clara a favor. Don't show him any houses in Santa Clara."

"What do you mean?"

"Persuade him to buy out of town. There's an area in San Jose that he liked. Show him around that area and around Willow Glen; just keep him the hell out of Santa Clara."

Sure enough, Mr. San Jose found a nice home in San Jose, except that he didn't have all the money to buy it. Not only did the real estate broker assist his move out of Santa Clara, but it was thought at the time that he and his father loaned Mr. San Jose the extra money needed to close the deal. Mr. San Jose was now living out of town when at a City Council meeting he started spouting off about Santa Clara's future and how adverse the stadium deal would be for residents. I queried him, "Excuse me, sir, but don't you live in San Jose?"... "Next speaker to the podium, please."

PROTECTING THE FAMILY JEWELS

Almost always you'll find me working, serving, enjoying Santa Clara's Annual Arts & Wine Festival in Central Park, a large and highly popular event. But in 2009 the festival took on a serious tone as politics, specifically Measure J–the 49ers Stadium initiative, took center stage. Among the booths of arts & crafts and food & drink were tables that stood out–those FOR and AGAINST the stadium, manned by the most fervent. I was hoping to have a good time at the festival; in fact I was so burned out from the politicking that all I wanted was to chill with a cold micro-brew from the beer tent. That's when I saw something that raised my temperature on this already warm afternoon. An operative was soliciting fair-goers and spewing out false information on the 49ers Stadium deal.

I approached him hoping to enlighten him. Our talk became a debate, civil at first. "I have first-hand knowledge of the facts, call City Hall if you don't believe me; you're giving out inaccurate information."

He became frustrated, suddenly raised his right knee and jammed it into my crotch! My left testicle took the weight of the blow and I winced painfully. I was shocked. It was no longer politics, it was mano-a-mano. I said, "If you ever touch me again, I'm going to knock you out."

"Are you threatening me?" he manned up.

"No, I'm making you a promise that if you ever get near me again, I'm going to take you down. That's not a threat; it's a promise." After that moment I never saw him at City Hall again.

STUDENT BECOMES THE TEACHER

While the City's efforts to bring the Giants and the Athletics to the South Bay provided experience, insight, protocols and infrastructure; Council and community members feared a repeat of the frustrations and empty results. At the center of stadium financing were Redevelopment Funds and the "Mello Roos" Hotel Tax. Mello Roos enabled Community Facilities Districts to be established by local government as a means of obtaining funding. Counties and cities use these financing districts to pay for public projects. The various funding sources were moving the deal toward safeguards for City resources and finances.

Nonetheless, the opposition was tossing out big cost numbers that were inaccurate. As the 49ers' deal kept getting better, they'd come up with another argument. I decided, to the curiousity of fellow Council members, to meet one-on-one with opposition leader Darth J-Hater. My tactic was to gain information from him; I figured if I was taking him out for breakfast or spending time with him, I diminished his time to work on the opposition. I wouldn't say we became good friends, but despite our difference of opinion, we got along surprisingly well.

Consultants play a valuable role so we pretty much hired them all in a full-court press. Unlike the previous campaigns where I had to come up with the money, we had four million dollars to run this campaign. Take four million dollars and divide it by 44,000 registered voters and you have a nice war chest. We spent it wisely. We went house-to-house, door-to-door, and even John York initially and Jed York later engaged in several house chats. I led a few, the more contentious ones it seemed.

One chat at the house of Susan T, with whom I'd worked on the Giants campaign, had a gathering that was unbelievable, I mean this was the Ritz Carlton Buffet. There were two contentious individuals raising their objections. Not wanting the festive affair affected by negativity, I took them aside personally to address their concerns with a buffet of political facts. These two professors thought they knew it all. From my Master's program work I was prepared to deal with professors. When they raised objections to a stadium in the north zone, I asked, "Well, what's your plan?"

"What do you mean?" one asked.

"What do you propose for developing the area?" I asked rhetorically before the clincher: "Do you think the NFL is going to be around in 50 years? Do you think the NFL will lose its popularity?" I felt quite certain that these two professors who were opposing the project now saw the decision in a different light.

Longtime buddy Pat with his daughter were lucky enough to be on the cover of the 2011 Season Ticket handbook.

Traffic was always the number one worry in house chats and community meetings. We sought conciliation in the fact that game traffic was limited to relatively few of the 365 days a year, most of those Sunday afternoons. Other points of discussion were around redevelopment of this industrial area, and, naturally, streams of revenue. Given the the amount of money allocated by both the 49ers and the NFL, Santa Clara scored an ideal package that included benefits to community.

The gods of finance came through before the venue even opened. The Niners and our Mission City struck gold with a new coach and winning seasons as ticket sales soared with the team's success.

THE LITTLE VENETIAN BLIND

In the spring preceding the June 2010 election, the nature of our City Council meetings began to change. Opposition groups showed up locked and loaded, ready to tear into us. And just the same, stadium boosters showed up not quite as angry, but instantly recognizable in their 49er hats and jerseys. They were there to support their position with equal force. The Council generally controlled the uproar, but there was always a lot of booing and hissing. I remember sitting on the council dais, looking out at the jam-packed meeting room, when the magnitude of what we were trying to accomplish finally struck me. If we succeed in building a stadium, it was going to change Santa Clara, change the entire Bay Area. So much was at stake, I had a tinge of empathy for those who feared change to our city. But progress moves us forward.

Before one such council meeting we were tipped off that a blind lady was going to speak in opposition. A blind lady? How the heck do you go against a blind lady? I knew this lady to be an outspoken type, but I always got along with her. Sadly, she came armed with bogus facts fed by the opposition, yet she would have had the audience's sympathy. The Pro Stadium supporters were concerned, but I assured them: "Don't worry, we have an older blind lady, and she's better." Her name was Glorian. I'd known her and her husband for years. She told me she was Venetian and that her husband used to call her affectionately "his little venetian blind." So after their lady spoke for the opposition, we brought up Glorian. Glorian was about 80 at the time. We helped her out of her seat. Glorian walked with a cane slowly up to the front of the assembly. The room was jam-packed, standing room only, but you could hear a pin drop. And you could practically hear what the opposition was thinking. "Shit, they've got a blind lady too?" Glorian did not disappoint. She showed a genuine passion for a 49ers Stadium. She was the last blind lady standing.

OPERATION MOM'S APPLE PIE

The most important prerequesite for the 49ers stadium was passage of the Santa Clara Ballot Measure J, an advisory vote by the citizens of Santa Clara. So the wording of that ballot measure had to be precise. The language alone could determine their votes of the undecideds. Following a City committee drafting of the ballot, key movers and shakers received copies. I wasn't among them; I preferred to leave the draft to the committee so I could focus on the other Niners issues. When Larry MacNeil received the draft ballot language he called me in a bit of angst, and told me he was coming over to my office.

I said, "How does it look? Is there a problem?" I feared.

Larry made it perfectly clear that we're screwed, absolutely screwed. We sat down together in a room with no windows, fitting because we felt like we were imprisoned by language that would doom us. Desperation all over his face, Larry looked like he'd lost his best friend. The ballot wording was not as bad as he made it out to be, but there was a lot missing. It made no mention of the money that the Niners had agreed to give to seniors, to parks and recreation, and the like. It should have included the perks, details that had every right to be printed in the Measure and would be helpful to the cause. The omissions had to be an oversight as I had provided such language to the committee. Even though I was not on the committee, I told Larry that I'd do my best to get the language changed.

Surprisingly, Larry resisted the offer; it was too late to change the ballot.

"No, it's not. I'll go talk to the City Manager."

He told me not to talk to the City Manager and stared me down. Larry was upset that the ballot language did not include more of the benefits to the community.

Larry voiced a legitimate and sensitive concern. But the rebel in me was of another mind and thought "As soon as you leave here I don't give a damn what you think or say, I'm going to get this ballot verbiage changed."

I jumped in my car and drove over to City Hall to talk with the City Manager, who was now leaning towards the stadium and aggressively working the deal. The City Manager was good about letting me meet with her, so I was at ease going into her office to talk this matter through. When I pointed out that the ballot measure was incomplete and might be challenged by savvy supporters, she took interest in what I had to say: "Wouldn't the ethical thing be to state the truth?"

By the end of the hour she agreed to change the language accordingly. The wording now read like a best seller that tugged at the hearts of America: "Do you love baseball, hot dogs, mom's apple pie, and Chevrolet?...and a cold beer on a hot day?"

With the partially rewritten ballot language in hand I headed over to the home of Jamie Matthews who was on the ballot committee. We were also joined by a not-to-be named individual skilled in writing language for ballot measures. I told Matthews we needed to change the ballot language. He was concerned about making any changes.

I showed him the draft. "See this," I said, "and do you see the name at the top of the stationery?" Jamie saw the City Manager's name and lit up knowing he had her approval on many points. He took the document from me and scanned over it. We rewrote that bitchin' ballot and it was beautiful. To this day, I cherish the memory that Larry MacNeil hung the new ballot measure right by his office door, and gave me credit for the wording, even though I had ignored his advice.

MEASURE J BALLOT MEASURE: This is the question that was presented to voters: Shall the City of Santa Clara adopt (Ordinance 17.20) leasing City property for a professional football stadium and other events; no use of City General or Enterprise funds for construction; no new taxes for residents for stadium; Redevelopment Agency funds capped for construction; private party pays all construction cost overruns; no City/Agency obligation for stadium operating/maintenance; private party payment of projected fair market rent; and additional funds for senior/youth/library/recreation to City's General Fund?

WHAT GOES UP, MUST COME DOWN–NOT NECESSARILY

As the election for a 49ers stadium drew near, the opposition found yet another issue. I knew from my work on the Saratoga/San Tomas Aquino Creek Trail that runs alongside the site that this argument was built on a mound of bullshit so deep it would take a month of Sundays to uncover it. But the opposition took advantage of the trail's popularity and posted fliers up and down the path stating that the trail would be closed 50 times a year. Fact: Only the trail adjacent to the Stadium would be closed, and not every weekend but only on major event days for security reasons.

Silicon Valley Business Ink - Trailblazers tap $20M

"Kevin Moore helped drive this 12-mile trail that runs through Intel's campus." March 9, 2001 By Lynn Graebner (Photo Credit Scott Lewis)

We sent out a couple of college kids from our campaign but they didn't find the fliers. So Jamie Matthews who also worked hard to build the trail and I drove out and we found them. We were about to rip them down because there's no posting allowed along the trail; but then we came up with an idea. What if we modified the flier in our favor? So allowing this brief exception to the rule, we made up a flier that read "Save the Creek Trail with money from the 49ers!" Trail-users pro or con went about their business as usual until one day an opponent stopped to read his work and almost had a heart attack–his message had turned against him!

Save the Trail, NO on J

68,500 Fans, 50 Times a Year, for 40 years

Every weekend this trail will be closed.

City Council is aware of this and refuses to take any action to protect the trail.

Bicyclists Beware

The "49er Stadium Draft Environmental Imapct Report (DEIR)" page 159, section 4.8.3.3 Background Bicycle and Pedestrian Facilities

"There are no planned or approved improvements to bicycle or pedestrian facilities within the project area. Nor are there any bicycle facilities planned according to the City of Santa Clara Transportation Bicycle Network."

San Tomas Aquino Creek Trail closed 50 times a year.

The Trail was built by local, county, State, and Federal tax dollars for safe access around major roads. This trail was not built to facilitate NFL fans on game day.

Save the Trail, NO on J

WALKING PRECINCTS ... SHOUTING THE FULL MONTY

Die hard Measure J stadium supporters gave their "soles" walking precincts. Most notable trekkers were Mayor Patricia Mahan, Councilman Jamie Matthews, and former Council Member Lisa Gillmor. Lisa shared with me that Jamie was worried about walking for "J" out of concern for his upcoming mayoral race and was extremely on edge in neighborhoods with the yellow anti-stadium signs. I told Jamie he needed to be out there, "If you're not walking for the stadium, you're not going to have people walking for you for Mayor, so you should get your ass out there." We were canvassing near Central Park, a typical Santa Clara neighborhood of tree-lined streets and working-class folk. As a kid I rode my bike through this neighborhood on my way to St. Justin School, so it was a friendly flashback.

You always expected some negative reactions and to encounter citizens who gave you a hard time just because you were in city government and were supposed to have solved every problem. But early on, the precinct canvassing was going pretty well. Then a '60s muscle car pulled up alongside the curb.

No one walked more for Jamie's Mayor's race than Trudy and I.

"Hey Jamie," beckoned some guy like he knew him well. "Jamie Matthews, come over here." Jamie walked over and leaned down toward the open passenger-side window. The crazy driver shouts: "go f-- yourself." As the crazy man sped off, Jamie looked stunned; he lost all motivation to walk.

We had almost finished that precinct, so I said, "Let's get the hell out of here." I knew a lot of people there who supported our efforts, but Matthews had lost his will to walk this street. "Let's walk another part of town," I suggested. I knew an area off Bowers Avenue by the old fire station. Polling indicated that with the exception of one nearby street the area was inclined to support Measure J. I directed us down the safe street, leapfrogging us from one house to the next. That's when poor Jamie got his second shock of the afternoon. Across the street a guy comes running out of his house into his yard and yelled, "Hey Matthews." Jamie turned and looked and the guy yelled: "Get the f-- out of my neighborhood. Get the f-- out of here."

Jamie glanced over at me and I gave him a "what the f--?" gesture and we both looked at the guy across the street standing boldly in his yard. He was naked, the Full Monty. We were relieved when we got back to Matthews' house. I sipped lemonade on Jamie's porch, we all laughed about the afternoon as Jaime just kept shaking his head in disbelief.

WHAT? KEVIN MOORE IS A PARTY POOPER!

I am always up for a good party – I love to dance and sing. Now the campaign was in high gear and going well. I decided one warm night to take a late drive by Measure J headquarters. The office was a storefront in the former Mervyns Plaza next to a Chinese restaurant, formerly JR Chops where I was hired years ago to lead the Santa Clara Giants effort. What to my surprise do I see but the young campaign staff drinking, dancing, carousing, having a good ol' time! Normally I would be cool with this, as long as their partying was discreet and not in the public view.

Measure J Awesome Campaign Staff

But no, booze was flowing, bodies were moving, the party was raging in storefront windows for all to see and next door to Baskin Robbins where families were exiting, ice-cream in hand. This public behavior pissed me off to no end. I charged through the open door and lectured these college students and grads like I was a Marine drill sergeant. For dramatic affect I grabbed a chair and tossed it á la Coach Bobby Knight. Our campaign theme promoted good family entertainment, and this was not it. I broke up the party but left them one consolation – they could rage at the Victory Party…and I'd join them in the celebration!

TWAS THE NIGHT BEFORE ELECTION AT THE MOORE'S

Shuttle diplomacy had been demanding; politicking had been stressful. Yet if the ballot measure passed, there was more of the same to come. Fearing a repeat of my total involvement as was the case with the Giants, I could easily find myself in the doghouse with my wife. But the stage was set, the play had begun.

I had been burning the midnight oil several weeks straight and I came home exhausted, needing some sleep before going back out to put up more Measure J yard signs and to pass out more literature. I walked in the door and Julee immediately confronted me, "We need to talk."

Loving my wife, I grabbed both of her hands and said, "Honey, I love you, but I cannot talk right now, I need to get 20 minutes of sleep." Our little dog, Trudy, was on the floor between us, almost as if she were taking it all in. So when I exited into the bedroom and fell upon the bed, Trudy came and cuddled up next to me; I needed the support. It was a short and convoluted sleep. I slept 20 minutes, rallied back up, and got up for one last all nighter.

George Netto in the middle of the night, navigating us to lawn sign locations.

Best donuts in the world after a long night of campaign work.

THE HEART OF ROCK 'N' ROLL IS STILL BEATING...BARELY!

The campaign to move forward with the stadium election was in its last days. It was managed in part by Ed McGovern, a political consultant whom I knew well, having battled him in other campaigns where he gained my respect. The pressure was intense. Every moment counted, and I'd slept only a few hours in the last three days. Twenty-one days of outstanding polling data was showing that we should win the Santa Clara 49ers stadium election by a good margin. Then came news that might as well have been delivered by The Grim Reaper, the kind of news that could put any political consultant into cardiac arrest. And it did! Thursday before the election, new polling data showed we were on the verge of losing. I conversed with Ed shortly after he received the adverse news, Ed is usually "Joe Montana cool."

Ed McGovern

To put this in context, I digress… Ed had worked on the original San Francisco Giants ballpark measure. With San Francisco Mayor Art Agnos, he was credited for recommending the China Basin location for the Giants' beautiful new ballpark. That election could not lose without a disaster of Biblical proportion. Well how about a 6.9 earthquake! That's exactly what happened at 5:04 pm on October 17th, 1989, before the A's-Giants World Series Game 3. Now some 20 years later, was Ed going to lose an election yet again in the final days? Ed told me that Friday morning he paced around the house so much he wore out the carpet and he began experiencing severe heart pains. His wife rushed him to the hospital. The emergency room doctor had to administer electrocardio shock therapy twice. By the grace of God, Ed survived. Diagnosed with heart palpitations, he was released from the hospital that afternoon. He returned home and promptly checked the new polling data.

"Winners, I am convinced, imagine their dreams first. They want it with all their heart and expect it to become true. There is, I believe, no other way to live." – Joe Montana, 49ers Hall of Fame Quarterback

EVERY VOTE COUNTS ... EVEN THE DRUNK LADY'S VOTE

Coming down to the wire, the polling numbers told us that it was going to be tight, and every single vote counted. Some races in Santa Clara were lost by a few votes. I was committed to finding every last one of those votes. I suggested that we canvas out by Wilcox High School to look for more votes. Santa Clara has the privilege of being one of the safest small cities in the country, but even here there are pockets of desperation. As we drove to that particular area of town, you could sense it. Dogs barked from front yards, lawns were unkept, paint pealed from the structures. One could imagine the illegal activities taking place between the narrow apartments.

Accompanying me was, I thought, a gentle soul, a recent transplant from Connecticut nicknamed "the Hippie Man." I don't think he felt as desperate as I did with only 28 minutes until the polls closed, but he obviously favored the stadium enough to walk precincts. We stumbled across this lady on the front porch drinking beers, already a little drunk. We talked with her and she said that she wanted to vote, chugging the last of her beer and stumbling toward her car.

"Ma'am," I said, "I'm not sure you want to drive in the condition you're in. How 'bout we drive you over there."

We drove to her polling station. She stumbled out of the car and somehow managed to cast her vote (for the stadium, hopefully!), then we drove her back. With no time left to vote, we were walking back to the car. We overheard from someone at the polling station that the vote was not going in our favor. The Hippie Man was so frustrated by the constant haranguing of the opposition that when we passed a yard with a "NO on J" sign, he grabbed it and flung it like a Frisbee.

"Don't do that," I reprimanded him, "that's not cool."

"The campaign is over," he said, "what does it matter." But it mattered to me, win or lose.

BIG BOYS DON'T CRY–WELL, MAYBE A LITTLE

I dropped the Hippie Man off at his apartment. Polls were now closed. Exhausted and discouraged, I headed down San Tomas Expressway back to campaign headquarters. Traffic was gridlock inching slowly toward El Camino Real where I stopped for the red light. What a heartbreak this defeat would be for all involved; we had come so far, we had come so close. My dream was *almost* a reality. In this moment of truth I got a phone call from Ed McGovern. "Kev," he said, "can you hear me okay?"

"Yeah?" I prayed that he was going to give me some good news... or was this to be the nail in the coffin?

"We won!" he shouted.

"Huh?" I said. "It's 8:10 and the polls have just closed."

"The absentee ballots are in and counted," Ed exclaimed. "We won, Kev, we won! There's no f--ing way they're going to catch us."

"But it's only 8:10," I repeated, disbelieving we could have won.

"Kev, it's over, we won!" he assured me again.

Having slept little those past few weeks, my emotions were frayed. I started crying profusely, tears swelled in my eyes, rolled down my cheeks. I have rarely cried so deeply. Thank God it was a long stoplight. I looked at the truck next to me; the driver was wearing a baseball cap. He looked over and saw me crying. He must have thought my wife just left me or something. He actually looked concerned. I put up my arm and motioned thumbs up "they're tears of joy." The guy gave me an "oh, okay" kind of nod. I pulled over to call my wife to share the news and to tell her to get ready for the election night victory party. There was no point in returning to campaign headquarters now. I headed home to my wife with the good news and to get ready for an election night PARTY!

ONE DOG NIGHT AT THE AMERICAN LEGION HALL

By the time I arrived home my tears of joy had subsided. I was floating on air. My wife Julee was dressed up, ready and waiting to attend the evening's victory party event, happy for me, relieved for us both. She put our dog in her "condo" in preparation for our departure.

"No worry, she's coming with us."

"Are you serious?"

"You bet I am," I said. "This dog is a superstar, she cuddled with me when I needed comfort; she walked precincts with me, she was with me this whole time. I'm true to my people including my pet! Trudy deserves to be there."

Julee accepted the inevitable, combing out the dog's hair and fluffing it up, making her look like one good lookin' poodle. Seeing Trudy primped for a grand premier was hilarious. But I also had an ulterior motive for bringing Trudy; she would be my diversion to the press. I'd done more than my share of interviews to this point, and tonight was not about interviews, it was about celebrating.

My wife and I arrived at the party with Trudy under my arm. Trudy sniffed around the middle of this big gathering and was a good pooch. It seemed like she knew she deserved to be there. As she sensed the increasing excitement, she pranced around like a rock star dog!

The election party was in a small, local American Legion Hall on Homestead Road across from Santa Clara University. It was exactly what you'd imagine an American Legion Hall to be, with lots of old folding chairs scattered about and patriotic memorabilia on the walls surrounding a large American Flag. A band played '50s tunes, kind of a Bebop medley, mixed with a little bit of Country. Then quite suddenly a flood of people flowed in. The

Niners brass arrived and were greeted with a chorus of cheers. The owners, John and Jed York, looked more relieved than happy. I could now joke with Ed that, while serious, his heart palpitations incident resembled the Jack Nicholson heart-attack scene in *Something's Got To Give.*

Jed York and my sister Emmy

Truly the campaign had been stressful on everyone. County Assessor Larry Stone who worked on several campaigns with me showed up; I made sure Larry was acknowledged for his assistance. The Campaign Committee honored council members with blue and gold Superman Capes that we all dawned that evening. They gave Lisa Gillmor a military jacket because she was in the trenches with us, and they had select gifts for other special contributors.

The media was all over the crowd, but unlike before when I was at their beck and call, taking every opportunity to garner support, tonight I didn't need to say a word. We had won the election and the last thing I wanted to do was give an interview. They were barking up the wrong tree, if they wanted commentary they could talk to my four-legged pal Trudy!

Council opposition member Will Kennedy, speaking from off-site appeared on the hall television. Some in the crowd booed him. He said the voters had spoken and he promised to support the initiative. I was proud of him for saying that and could now count on his skills to help finalize details of the stadium operations.

As election night coverage wore on, many including the *San Francisco Chronicle* noted that the "Gavin Newsom for Lieutenant Governor Party" had a 10-piece band playing in the State Capitol; while here in Santa Clara, Measure J celebrants had a '50s rock band playing in an old America Legion Hall – but we could have the Niners playing in the Mission City.

"It's not the size of the dog in the fight, it's the size of the fight in the dog."
-- Mark Twain, Novelist

4th Quarter

Photo by Michael Fallon

PASS THE PARMESAN CHEESE

The 49ers stadium deal was in our hands, but the game wasn't over. When I recovered from the night of celebrating, I realized that we were no better off than San Francisco had been after the voters had approved a stadium complex for the 49ers–that Stadium Mall was never built. Either my beloved 49ers or my beloved City could derail the will of the people. No sooner had I come to that conclusion then the phone started ringing. Yes, the conversations had changed tenor, but the pressure only ratcheted up as we scrambled to finalize loose ends of the deal and plan the construction of a professional sports stadium.

The stadium deal was tied in part to Santa Clara redevelopment funds. But with the Great Recession impacting the State budget, Governor Brown enacted cuts to the funds. This created a crisis for us. I decided we needed to meet quickly and the meeting would have to be only three council members to avoid violating the Brown Act.

So, Councilwoman Lisa Gillmor, now-Mayor Jamie Matthews and I had a meeting with Larry MacNeil at By-Th'-Bucket Bar & Grill, a popular family-run establishment in Santa Clara. Mayor Matthews was concerned, over the nature of this meeting. Having been served his pasta dish as the discussion warmed up, he grabbed a shaker of Parmesan cheese, unscrewed the lid, and poured the shaker over his dish. We strived to figure out how to start construction on the staduim despite the Governor's cuts to the redevelopment funds. The Mayor wanted to postpone any decision, but mindful of San Francisco's debacle in their attempt to build a stadium, I was nervous about slowing the momentum. I did not want to repeat San Francisco's mistakes; I recommended that we start construction as soon as possible.

"How can you build a billion dollar stadium without major funding?" I was asked. "It's an insane idea," I was told. It feels like I'm being driven back into my own end zone. But there doesn't seem like much of an option here; we've got to go for it.

"Even if the Niners don't end up locating here, we'll still have infrastructure in place for the future," I reasoned. As the discussion intensified the Mayor became more agitated. He grabbed another shaker of Parmesan, unscrewed the lid and emptied the entire container over his food. The pasta disappeared; all you could see was cheese, one big mountain of cheese.

At that point a fellow council member showed up at our table. "Hey, what are you three doing here?" I stated the obvious, "Having lunch."

The Mayor's face turned pale, as if he'd seen a ghost. The expression on his face read to get him the hell out of there. We quickly dismissed our fellow councilman.

When our associate left I persisted, "We've got to invest the redevelopment money. The State government is not going to stop an active construction site during a recession. And if there's no stadium, we'll build an office park like the opposition is proposing." Pondering this proposal over their pasta, my colleagues coalesced behind an action later with the full council supporting using redevelopment money to get the project moving forward. The stadium deal was impregnated by spending our redevelopment dollars on further infrastructure. At long last we were taking our first real concrete steps.

WHEN THE LIGHTS GO DOWN IN THE CITY

It might have been the 4th quarter, but the game was far from over. San Francisco stepped up to make a final push to save the Niners. Carmen Policy, former CEO, was enlisted by the City in hopes his influence could persuade the 49ers to give San Francisco a second chance. Even though Santa Clara passed the Measure, Carmen protested that such a little town could not possibly finance such a big stadium. He swore that Hunters Point was still the better location. Then, as if by divine intervention, the God of Light decided to settle it once and for all; God pulled the plug on San Francisco.

On December 19, 2011, the Pittsburgh Steelers were to play the 49ers at Candlestick Park on Monday Night Football. The game was billed as a great match-up of two playoff bound teams–until the lights went out. Twenty minutes prior to kick-off, the stadium lights shuttered down until the entire stadium and its sellout crowd of 69,000 was left in the dark. "It *was* dark," Coach Harbaugh affirmed. Twenty minutes later power was restored, only to have another transformer blow thereafter, sending the stadium once again into blackness. If Jed York needed proof to convince the NFL that its $150 million contribution to a new Santa Clara stadium would be well spent, he could hardly have picked a starker example.

"During the lengthy Monday outages, in fact, one Santa Clara booster was quietly smiling" wrote **Mark Purdy, in the Mercury News.** "Santa Clara Councilman Kevin Moore said the city's independent energy company, Silicon Valley Power, has a reliability rating that ranks in the top quartile nationally."

Football viewers were upset by the downtime while watching the primetime game, but not me. With one of the best utilities in the West, owning its own electricity grid, Santa Clara just had the deal sealed.

I had to laugh when Facebook exploded with comments like: "Kev, you blew out that transformer, admit it."

A pic sent to me from the Movie Airplane wher Stephen Stucker uplugs the runway lights.

The funniest follow-up was a letter typed on an official San Francisco Agency letterhead. "A 1968 light yellow Firebird bearing Santa Clara license plates was seen leaving the site of the blown transformer."

In turned I posted a still frame from the movie *Airplane* of a a guy unplugging the runway lights with a caption that read "Just kidding." I know this was no joke to San Francisco. A new Santa Clara stadium quickly gained momentum. The Candlestick wick was burning out. The Niners had to build a new stadium and build it soon. The blackout accelerated the timetable by a year.

Let there be light … Genesis 1:3

THE SLEEPER PLAY

With the use of redevelopment funds still in question, and with City of San Francisco officials amping up a last ditch effort to keep the team, several council members felt it was time to quickly call an audible – another EMERGENCY MEETING. We attempted to contact Mayor Jamie Matthews to make the call. It was becoming clear that the Mayor did not want to call such a meeting. We surmised that he did not want to upset the City Manager who had a firm hand on the deal. After numerous attempts to reach the Mayor, it was time to take matters into our own hands and that's just what we did. A trio of council members went into the City Manager's office and suggested calling for the emergency meeting.

The Mayor explained later the reason he could not be reached was that he was getting some much needed sleep during our desperate attempts to contact him. With the Mayor now rested, he was on his A game. That emergency meeting was critical to our efforts to move construction forward and put people to work.

FINAL DRIVE RUNNING OUT THE CLOCK

My love of sports had turned into a labor of love this past decade. And now that momentum was decisively building for the 49ers, I was glowing with anticipation and excitement for the 2012 football season and beyond. While the work was unrelenting, the City of Santa Clara was humming, gaining yardage month by month. The game was in control, the clock was running down on the City of San Francisco and on the local opposition. The media barrage lightened and the drive was receiving positive press. A series of offensive plays by our team continued to advance the ball toward the end zone and ultimate victory. The drive sequence:

"Today I will do what others won't, so tomorrow I can accomplish what others can't." – Jerry Rice, 49ers Hall of Fame Receiver

MARCH 2011. The Santa Clara City Council would decide whether to stash $4.5 million in redevelopment funds with the 49ers for a proposed football stadium if the State persisted in its attempt to disband all groups intending redevelopment funded projects.

JUNE 2011. Committee of the Whole study session took place to provide an update to Council and the public on the status of the stadium project, specifically in the areas of the stadium lease, structure, stadium management, and Disposition and Development Agreement and financing plan.

JULY 2011. Richard Robinson, Robinson Communications, Consultant to the 49ers, posted a Facebook message. RE: City Manager Recommendation:

"Simple greed, whether by a business or a city is usually not the best policy. The quality of a project, the character of the business people and the intangible assets a project may possess can and should trump simple short-term dollars and cents. The City is on strong financial footing, not because we made decisions based on the immediate highest dollar bids, but because we made sound long-term investments with people and entities who want to help and improve our City. This is such a project."

DECEMBER 2011. After two public Study Sessions on December 6 and 8, the Santa Clara Stadium Authority approved a Disposition and Development Agreement between the Stadium Authority and the 49ers Stadium Company, which is the overall legal structure of the Stadium Project.

JANUARY 2012. A day after election officials verified a stadium opposition group's petition to put the stadium project back on the June election ballot, the Santa Clara City Council voted 5-2 to reject the referendum. Said Councilman Pat Kolstad, "if all our votes could be referend-able (sic), the will of the people would never get done. Fifty-eight percent of city voters approved the stadium project in a June 2010 election. Don't these people ever give up! How much convincing does it take to show that a 49er Stadium deal is the best thing that one could ever imagine for Santa Clara and its future. We *can* have it both ways: we can remain a small city and invest in our future for years to come."

FEBRUARY 2012. National Football League owners approved $200 million in a G-4 loan that would be directed to fund construction costs for the new stadium in Santa Clara, the new home for the San Francisco 49ers.

The approval was the last piece of financing needed for construction to begin on the stadium, and the 49ers were the first franchise to receive support from the new stadium fund that was crafted in the collective bargaining agreement with NFL players last year. "With the NFL's muscle now behind the new stadium, we are moving forward," said Jed York, CEO of the 49ers. "I expect an official groundbreaking ceremony very soon. Get your hard hats ready; we are embarking on the path to the next generation of 49ers football."

FEBRUARY 2012. Santa Clara City Council approved a Ground Lease between the City and the Santa Clara Stadium Authority for City-owned property to be developed for a professional football Stadium.

MARCH 2012. Financing of the 1.3 billion project was formalized.

APRIL 2012. The SF 49ers Santa Clara Stadium Newsletter printed *An Important Update*. "Less than two years ago, the 49ers shook hands with the citizens of Santa Clara on an exciting plan to build a new stadium....But our mutual agreement was about more than a stadium….It was about jobs. Thousands of them. It was about an economic boost for local businesses. More funding for schools. And ironclad protections for Santa Clara taxpayers….While the stadium begins a new chapter in our relationship with Santa Clara, we want every aspect of the project to remain an open book to Santa Clarans. We want you to know with certainty that the new stadium project will meet or exceed every commitment made to the citizens of Santa Clara."

MARCH 2012. The San Francisco 49ers media team prepared a mailing for the upcoming Groundbreaking ceremony. The initial caption on the mailer was to read: "The dirt's about to fly in Santa Clara". When Kevin Moore saw this tag-line he went bonkers: "Are you frickin' crazy?!? You can't put that on your promo flier! With all due respect, this venture has already kicked up a lot of dirt on both sides. You don't want anymore dirt flying anywhere, not in Santa Clara, not in San Francisco, not anywhere.

How about something positive?" The new mailer read: "You're going to need this sooner than you think" … that being a construction hard hat which graced the cover. Inside the flier it stated: "The hard hats are ready to go at the new stadium in Santa Clara."

A GIFT FOR LLOYD

On April 19, 2012, ground for the new stadium was to be broken. There would be no turning back, no more negotiations, no reneging by the Niners. The media was primed to cover the event. The night before, Lloyd LaCuesta from Channel 2 News wanted an interview. I rallied the team. Patty Mahan was scheduled to attend a Sister Cities dinner, but I persuaded her to delay her engagement and join me. Despite ongoing cancer treatment, she showed up wearing a smile. We all met for an interview that was to take place at the top of the Great America Sky Tower, the same spot on which many years earlier we had sold the NFL Commissioner on Santa Clara's feasibility as an NFL site. We talked about our initial meeting with the Commissioner and Patty's tremendous job of showing off the Valley's delights. I took a backseat to the interview (one of the few times in my life I kept my mouth shut), letting Patty get the credit she well deserved. For these interviews we would do what is called a "walk-by"–walking separately by the camera. But I held her hand and we walked together.

After the Tower interview I had Lloyd follow me a short distance to the site where groundbreaking would take place. The area was cordoned off like Guantanamo Bay; *nobody* was allowed into the site, so carefully set for the big event. The grounds were dimly lit, secured by guards and video surveillance. I snuck Lloyd through the fencing into the makeshift arena, located the guard and identified myself and my purpose. Because Lloyd was leaving Channel 2 News after a stellar career, and because he had always given Santa Clara a fair shake, I wanted to give him a gift, an exclusive interview to beat the other stations. I phoned over to Niners headquarters figuring I'd catch someone making last-minute preparations, hoping for a 49ers officer worthy of an interview with Lloyd. I connected with a young woman rising fast in the organization. I explained the desire for an exclusive interview. She said she needed permission. I boldly stated, "I'm giving you permission and if there's flack I'll take the blame." She agreed and walked over to meet Lloyd who gave her a smile as wide as the Golden Gate Bridge. Lloyd's interview was superb, she communicated the message like a pro. The next day I informed the Niners of the importance of the interview and commended the officer. A few months later she was promoted.

GROUNDBREAKING - GET THAT SHOVEL IN THE GROUND

With Pat Kolstad and Lisa Gillmor

I could not sleep waiting for the next day to arrive. I was as a kid on Christmas Eve waiting to tackle that pile of presents under the Christmas Tree. I invited every person who had ever helped with the effort to build a 49ers stadium, and further invited old teachers, political allies, and every friend I could think of. I wanted them all to be there and share in this magnificent moment. The turning of a shovel of earth would signal that the dream I held most of my life was to become reality.

Ed McGovern, 49ers campaign consultant and friend, had arranged to drive me to the event. In Parking Lot A we linked up with my family, and friends who'd flown in from across the country. Organizers brought boosters in on a motorized cable car. Entering the arena gates, all attendees were given gold-trimmed construction hard hats with "SF" logos on the sides and wording 'round the brim: "New Santa Clara Stadium Groundbreaking April 19, 2012." The gold helmet topped off my suit; I and the other council members were dressed to the hilt. VIP badges dangled from around our necks.

A path of red carpet and velvet cords on gold stanchions led us into the makeshift arena framed by a stage and bleachers. Front stage was the focal point for the actual groundbreaking and the center of what would become the 49ers playing field. Behind was a huge stage with jumbo screen and towering speakers on either side. Facing the staging area were bleachers packed to the gills with whole families squeezed tightly together. The overflow crowd stood right and left of center. To the far left was the largest circus tent I'd ever seen, a hospitality area stocked with five-star food and beverages. Cheerleaders in

BREAKING GROUND IN SANTA CLARA

HNTB ARCHITECTURE

A full sectional rendering shows the 49ers' new stadium, which will seat 68,500 people and will cost $1.2 billion.

KICKOFF

PATRICK TEHAN/STAFF PHOTOS

Santa Clara Councilman Kevin Moore, from left, former Mayor Patricia Mahan, Mayor Jamie Matthews, 49ers Co-Chairwoman Denise DeBartolo York, 49ers CEO Jed York, 49ers Co-Chairman John York, Councilwoman Lisa Gillmor and Councilman Pat Kolstad break ground Thursday on the stadium.

49ers usher in new era with $1.2 billion stadium set to open in 2014

red & gold with shimmering pom-poms were lined up. Festive music played. The scene looked and sounded like a Hollywood premiere. Santa Clara had seen nothing quite like this, it was sheer excitement.

I walked up into the bleachers where campaign volunteers were seated. These "uncommon common" folk had worked so hard down in the trenches. I had a penchant for hanging out with them. No question, it was going to be exciting up on stage, but I wasn't done hugging and kissing all the people that helped us get there. While conversing with family, friends, and fans, I heard my name called over the loudspeaker system for the third time: "Will Kevin Moore please come up to the front of the stage...Will Kevin Moore please come to the staging area." I detoured from a desire to remain with family and friends and worked my way to the stage. I got there and Councilman Kolstad said to me, "Moore, where the hell were you?"

I said, pointing out to the bleacher crowd and joking, "Out there with hundreds of registered voters." At the staging area were Vernon Davis and Patrick Willis, stars of the 49ers. We chatted awhile. Then we each were introduced onto the stage, athletes coming into the arena. I was *one of them*–it was a unique experience. Ted Robinson, the 49ers announcer, did an excellent job announcing all the MVPs. I had never been introduced to such a large crowd before and in such a setting. Looking out over the throng of people, the feeling was fantastic. Each major VIP had a short speech to deliver. Mayor Jamie Matthews jokingly acknowledged me in his speech. The Mayor himself was full of excitement at being one of the leading speakers at this event. I personally had asked the 49ers to include former Mayor Patty Mahan at the podium, so she, too, could offer a few words, because she was so instrumental in leading the way in the beginning.

Jed York, CEO, San Francisco 49ers, then spoke: "The San Francisco 49ers organization has enjoyed a tremendous relationship with the City of Santa Clara and its citizens for more than 25 years. As community partners, we are very proud of all that has been accomplished in that span, and look forward to our new stadium serving as a testament to the passion for innovation shared by Santa Clara and the 49ers."

Before we left the stage we donned the red, white and gold hardhats most of the crowd wore atop their heads in the afternoon glow of the sun. We moved down from the stage to the actual groundbreaking plot on Mother Earth, a plot of land that was to become the 50-yard line, the epicenter of the future stadium. Then we VIPs took our choreographed positions around the traditional red and gold SF logo painted onto the ground, though all I could see from my close-up angle was a patch of red. We each carried with us a shovel. Its gold handle was inscribed "April 19, 2012," wood-burned onto its shaft was "Groundbreaking," and the glimmering gold spade was etched "FUTURE HOME OF THE SAN FRANCISCO 49ERS / NEW SANTA CLARA STADIUM," an insignia read "SCSA - Santa Clara Stadium Authority."

When I speared my gold-plated shovel into the ground and applied pressure with my foot, I sensed my leg locked with resistance, the ground was so fricking hard. (That exact spot had been a parking lot for years and you would have thought a ground crew could have softened up the clay a little better.) But geology aside, I made damn sure that my shovel blade broke the earth. In the *Mercury News* photo the next day, everybody is posed, looking up and so professional–but me; my head is bent. I'm intently looking down, pressing that golden tip as deep into the ground as I could, as if it were a personal triumph over previous failures. When I reflected on my pose in the photo, I thought I looked like Robin Williams' Mork from Ork leaning over and processing, "Nanu, nanu."

Suddenly the sky seemed to open and a cloudburst of red and gold confetti was flying all about in the breeze and descending upon us. A song struck up, blaring loudly out of the speaker towers, U2's *It's a Beautiful Day*, a perfect choice for the occasion and the weather. Still standing there at the birth spot of a professional sports stadium for which I had toiled so long, it was one of the proudest moments of my life. Thirty years of failure were erased. There were no more battles, the war was won, peace would finally come to this journey I called life.

I posed for an endless amount of pictures; everyone just kept clicking away. I knew that a food and drink party was kicking-off in the BIG TENT and I was thirsty, a little hungry, and more than a little ready to PARTY.

After more photos and handshakes and exchanges of congratulations, I wandered through the incredible block-long carnival-like food and drink tent, desperately searching for my wife Julee. In this absolutely huge party scene, finally I found her–Eureka! We embraced, I saw the most beautiful eyes in the world and gave Julee a big kiss. We soon connected with family, friends, high school pals, college buddies, associates past and present. All were there. The Miller family was there, a family of 12; and the McCarthy family

Into the End Zone with the 49ERS in Levi's Stadium

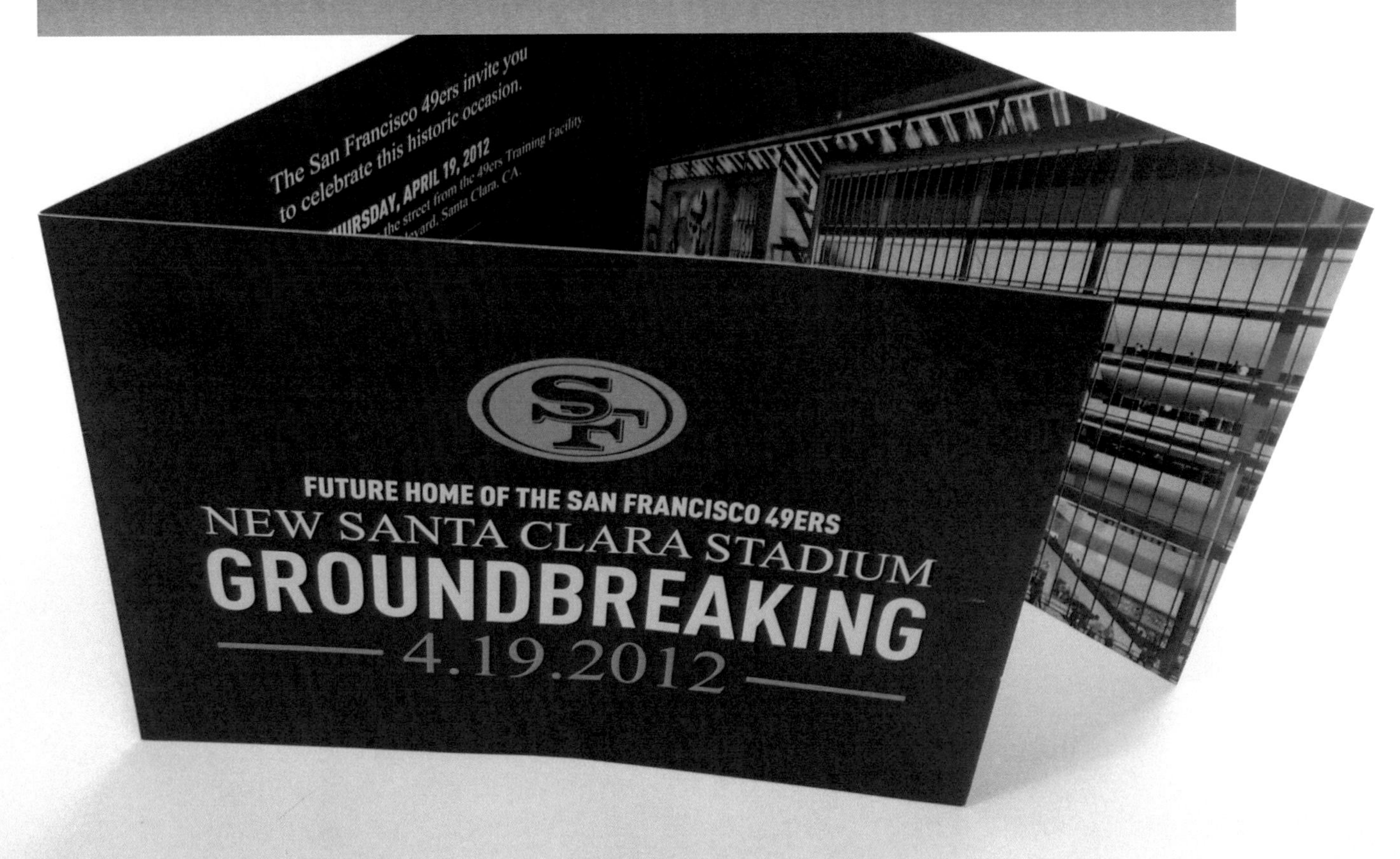

Mom, Dad, Sister Ann

Dick and Mike Saso with 49ers Gold Rush

With the McCarthy Brothers

With the Miller Family

of 13 was in rare form. The Miller and McCarthy brothers were parading the ceremonious shovel around the room like it was the Ark of the Covenant until it was time to pass the shovel off to the Moore sisters for a victory dance in an area that would eventually become a grass end zone. It was crazy, wonderful, fantastic. Julee and I wove our way through bodies to the dance floor. When the song *Shout* played I thought, "You know what? I'm gonna worm, I'm gonna gator." I hit the floor, I didn't care. I was on top of the world, albeit I was on the ground. This was the moment Santa Clara and I had waited for. Thank you, God!

THE ORIGINAL FORTY-NINER WEAR AND 50th NUGGET

Now that the 49ers Stadium was birthed, it needed a name. Naming Rights are a critical part of an event center's financial package. I had a heads-up that our stadium might be named Levi's. There were other names the 49ers turned down, and some that would have been controversial. Some organization even submitted a bid to name it "Pink Taco Stadium"–that was probably someone in the opposition. Such names were quickly dispatched. In short order came the bid by Levi's–all agreed it was a fine fit. Then came a surprise. Jed York phoned me on my birthday, May 7. "Kev, I have a birthday present for you. We've sold the Naming Rights. Our new home will be named Levi's Stadium." He disclosed the amount of the agreement. I was ecstatic about the name and the deal; and Jed's call on my birthday was a class jesture.

The next day the San Francisco 49ers announced that Levi Strauss & Co. had purchased naming rights to their stadium in Santa Clara, California. The naming rights deal called for Levi's to pay $220.3 million to the City of Santa Clara and the 49ers over 20 years with an option to extend the deal for another five years for around $75 million. The opposition had insisted we would get nowhere near the sponsorship dollars sought. This deal exceeded our projection.

Levi Strauss & Co. was founded in 1853 when Bavarian-born Levi Strauss moved to Gold Rush era San Francisco to open a dry goods business. He sold clothes, boots and other goods to the small retail stores of the American West.

San Jose Mercur

BAY AREA NEWS GROUP
2.7 MILLION BAY AREA READERS WEEKLY IN PRINT AND ONLINE

Thursday, May 9, 2013

SANTA CLARA STADIUM

49ers' fit: Levi's

BIG MONEY: Clothier to pay $220M for naming rights

ICONIC NAME: S.F. company has been around 140 years

About Levi's® Stadium

Levi's® Stadium is the new home to the San Francisco 49ers, and will also serve as one of the world's best outdoor sports and entertainment venues. It was designed by HNTB and was built by Turner/Devcon for the Santa Clara Stadium Authority. The $1.2 billion venue has 1.85 million square feet, seats approximately 68,500 and features 170 luxury suites and 9,000 club seats. It was designed to be a multi-purpose facility with the flexibility to host a wide range of events, including domestic and international soccer, college football, motocross, concerts and various civic events, and will be expandable for major events such as the Super Bowl. Levi's® Stadium is owned by the Santa Clara Stadium Authority, a public joint powers authority that was established to provide for development and operation of Levi's® Stadium to ensure that the stadium serves the goals of the City of Santa Clara. Visit www.LevisStadium.com.

I never really looked past the construction of the Stadium. Well, maybe I did imagine actually sitting in the stands and watching a 49ers football game in its opening season here in Santa Clara. It was a short distance but a far cry from first watching as a five-year-old a professional team play at Buck Shaw Stadium. But for Santa Clara and Levi's Stadium to be named host for the milestone 50th Super Bowl was beyond my wild imagination.

"Quality never goes out of style." – Levi Strauss

"Santa Clara's Levi's Stadium to host Super Bowl L!"

"Here it comes. The biggest, baddest sports spectacular in the United States of America. Super Bowl L–that is L as in roman numeral 50; and "L" as in "L"ove it–will be an unofficial national holiday. This is an extravaganza and event so special that it dwarfs all other sporting events... It started with a vision, a letter and a personal visit. Now former Santa Clara Vice Mayor Kevin Moore, a sports enthusiast, wrote a letter to the San Francisco 49ers describing his idea to build a new stadium in Santa Clara. It was a Hail Mary, but the 49ers were already headquartered in Santa Clara, the land was available, the weather is outstanding, the infrastructure and transit options first class, and Candlestick Park was a deteriorating joke."

Rich Robinson, SanJoseInside.com

Levi's Stadium Continues to be a Game Changer for Santa Clara with Super Bowl 50

The journey to hosting Super Bowl 50 started over seven years ago when Council Member Kevin Moore sent a letter to the NFL Commissioner requesting the NFL consider Santa Clara as the site for a new 49ers stadium. This request came in the middle of negotations the 49ers were having with the City of San Francisco that were not progressing. Kevin's letter could not have been better timed since it triggered the NFL and the 49ers to shift their focus to Santa Clara... The Chamber of Commerce is proud to have been a strong supporter of this transformational project and looks forward to continuing our support for continued economic growth around the stadium that Council Member Kevin Moore started over seven years ago.

Steve Van Dorn, CEO, Santa Clara Chamber of Commerce-May 2013

Julee with Jose Mezzettie and Team Fun!

GOOD BYE TO MY OLD FRIEND "THE STICK"

My good friend Rob Mezzetti invited Julee and me to the last tailgate he was hosting at "THE STICK" on July 12, 2014. Rob also scored us on-the-field VIP passes for the "Legends of Candlestick". The spirited Mezzetti family and friends did not disappoint, for they hosted a fun-filled tailgate with an incredible spread of food and beverages. Joining in the celebration was the beautiful and sweet Jennifer Montana and most of the Montana clan, minus Joe who was warming up for the Legends football game.

The 49er legends were slated to play a last flag football game at Candlestick Park against an All-Star team led by NFL Hall of Fame quarterback Dan Marino. The 49ers team was comprised of former Niner legends: Joe Montana, Ronnie Lott, Dwight Clark, Brent Jones, Jerry Rice, John Taylor, Dwight Hicks, Eric Wright, Tom Rathman, Charles Haley, Eric Davis, Mike Shumann, Jesse Sapolu, Keena Turner, Guy McIntyre, Bubba Paris, Roger Craig, and Steve Young among others.

The game was a smile-fest on and off the field. The players and fans were having a blast appreciating this very last game at the "The Stick." In all the excitement I could not resist making my move. Wearing my own 49ers jersey and befriending a security guard, I snuck my way onto the 49er Legends sidelines. I was able to mingle with the players and by a stroke of Candlestick magic, I ran into one of my all-time favorites, former 49ers Owner Eddie DeBartolo. Eddie D. and I shared some laughs. He was the same down-to-earth gentleman whom I enjoyed visiting with years ago.

The 49ers Legends won on the final play when Eddie DeBartolo caught a Joe Montana pass for the winning touchdown. Eddie D. spiked the ball and was hoisted up on the shoulders of his former players. A classic ending indeed!

On the drive home, dates and memories of The Stick flooded my mind. I recalled sneaking into the 49ers locker room, driving my car into the stadium, my friends detained by Candlestick Security and these memorable happenings:

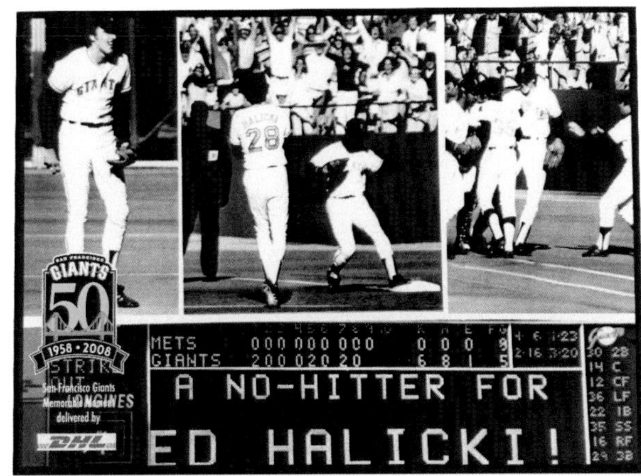

A Halicki NO-NO - August 24, 1975. Giants' left-hander Ed Halicki pitches a No-hitter.

KEVIN MOORE'S DAY OFF - April 9, 1982. My high school buddies Anthony, Tom, and I bailed on school and headed to The Stick for a sunny Giants Opening Day. We had no tickets and scoured the parking lot for a scalper. The ticket gods were with us, a San Francisco cop gave us three tickets that he confiscated from a scalper. Five minutes later a sharply dressed older man tapped me on the shoulder and offered us three more free tickets.We scalped three of those tickets, took the money and bought beer and peanuts.

A LAP DANCE AT THE NINERS GAME - December 29, 1984. My girlfriend and I went to watch the 49ers play the NY Giants in the NFC Divisional Playoffs. We were bummed when one of our tickets was a fake. Everything turned out fine, however, as the usher let my girlfriend sit on my lap. 49ers won 21-10. We jumped down onto the field in celebration, and then grabbed a handful of some of the end zone turf as a souvenir.

MONTANA'S LAST GAME AS A 49ER - Dec 28, 1992. Live on Monday Night Football, Joe throws his last touchdown pass as a 49er. I believe if the 49ers had kept Joe for one more season we would have six Super Bowl trophies.

RICE'S LAST GAME AS A 49ER - Dec 17, 2000. The view from my seat was obstructed by a large beam. (No beams obstruct any views at the new Santa Clara stadium). I had to lean over to watch the game. Terrell Owens set a record with 20 receptions. Jerry Rice the GOAT (Greatest Of All Time) is carried off the field, and 49ers win 17-0.

NINERS GO MARCHING IN - January 14, 2012. I take my buddy Mike Saso to his first 49ers playoff game against the New Orleans Saints. 49er quarterback Alex Smith completes a 14-yard pass to Vernon Davis with nine seconds left for a 36-32 win. One of the greatest playoff games ever.

Last look back at The Stick

SIR PAUL CLOSES DOWN "THE STICK"

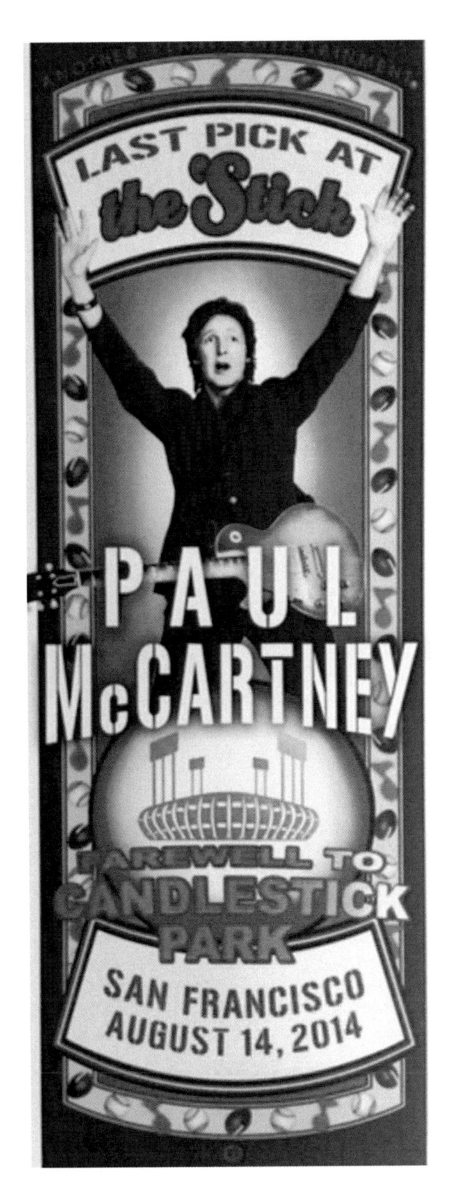

The most historic concert at Candlestick Park was surely when The Beatles performed their last official concert at the stadium on August 29, 1966. No one invited me (I was only two-years-old at the time), so when I heard that Sir Paul McCartney would be the headliner on the final gig at "The Stick" on August 14, 2014, I had to be there. I also knew my buddy Paul Miller, a huge Beatles fan, needed to be there with me.

As we arrived at the site and were working our way to the main parking lot, we quickly discovered that some buffoon had apparently closed all entrances to the parking lots while there were still empty parking spaces inside.

This was reconfirmed moments later when a car packed with young college women pulled up alongside us and one of them hollered "This is the third damn time we've circled this lot, we can't get in....What should we do? "

Next, we hear a man and woman (both with heavy Scottish accents) yelling at each other at the top of their lungs. The couple are illegally parked roadside and in heated discussion next to their 1960's vintage VW bus. In an irritated voice the woman yelled at the man: "You're not parking the car here illegally." The Scottish man quickly responded: "You bet your sweet ass I am, the van is staying right here!" The frustrated fellow then pulled out two enormous cushions from the back of the van, cushions that probably originated from an old living room couch. The woman then shouted out, "You are not taking those cushions in with us!" The scruffy Scot yelled back, "Hell yes, I am, and we are going to sit our asses on them and watch Paul f---ing McCartney!" Just when I thought I had seen it all from these two wild Scots, the old dude fired up a joint and started walking with his lady towards The Stick, while trying to manage the cumbersome cushions at the same time.

With Paul Miller

If they could park illegally, why couldn't we? That is when Miller and I decided to pull over and park wherever our car would fit. Illegal or not, for we needed to get inside. The music had already started. Sir Paul was on stage and we could hear the crowd rockin' to "Eight Days a Week." As we hopped out of the car, we were distracted again by the same college coed from earlier, and this time she screamed, "You guys are parking illegally?" I shouted back, "Yes." Then my buddy Miller decided to play parking official and proceed to yell at a series of frustrated drivers who've been circling outside the park like hornets, exclaiming, "If you ALL pull over and park, there is no way they would ticket us all."

Seconds later, dozens of cars joined us in a "closed parking lot protest" and, parked illegally. We marched toward The Stick, a band of parking rebels. But now Miller and I have another problem, we have no tickets. With the concert rocking with the amazing sound of familiar lyrics, we sought the scalpers, and quickly.

This time I am flush with cash. We passed on a few ticket offers from various scalpers, not expecting a scalper to take a check, and it paid off. A scalper approached us with an offer we couldn't refuse. Two tickets in a luxury suite with free beer and food. I said "Sold" and pass over the cash.

Paul McCartney was fantastic. He included all the tunes we enjoyed so much growing up. Returning from a trip to the Men's restroom, a group of security officers (resembling Secret Services agents) were approaching down the hallway. I was curious whom they might be protecting. Was it San Francisco's Mayor Lee? Could it be Yoko Ono? It was neither. Instead, there appeared Lieutenant Governor of California and former San Francisco Mayor Gavin Newsom. Up to this day, I'd never met my former stadium rival. Yet a subtle voice in my head encouraged me to walk up to my former political foe and greet him with respect. I stared right into his eyes, reached out my hand, and said, "Hello Gavin, I'm Kevin Moore from Santa Clara." He paused, and with a responsive handshake, Gavin said to me, "Good job." I respond, "Thank You." And we both went our separate ways.

My buddy Paul and I sang and danced through Paul McCartney's final set. We watched the fabulous fireworks display, then we exited The Stick for the very last time. As we reached our car we were amazed that it hadn't been towed nor ticketed. We also observed the horrendous amount of traffic attempting to exit and concluded that if we leave now, we'd move at a turtle's pace for the next couple hours. Instead, we started a post-concert party right there on the side of the road. We eventually left The Stick at 2:37am. That was the last hurrrah for The Stick.

"It's sad to see the old place closing down...but we're going to close it down in style." – Paul McCartney

RIBBON CUTTING AT THE FIELD OF JEANS

The formal invitation read "San Francisco 49ers of Levi's Stadium Ribbon-Cutting." Two years had already passed since the groundbreaking. For a variety of reasons I wanted to go with Lisa Gillmor, my "sister-in-arms". Coincidentally, Lisa, who was back on the Santa Clara Council, phoned to ask if I wanted to attend with her. Had she read my mind? "I'd love to go with you, Lisa." She was the perfect person to accompany. Being a twosome for this event felt right. We'd walk many a precinct together for Measure J, so why not hang out at the ribbon cutting too.

As we entered the Stadium we were directed through a media tent and then escorted over near a group comprised of the NFL Commissioner, Roger Goodell; San Francisco 49ers Owners, the York family; and several other 49ers executives. I wanted to give a "hello" to the Commish. I walked up one side of the entourage and attempted to ease myself through the photographers only to have the crush of the Press force me back. I circled around the other side and forced myself through like a Frank Gore run up the gut and said, "Hi, Mr. Goodell. Welcome back to Santa Clara. My name's Kevin Moore. I was up in the Sky Tower with you."

Roger Goodell reciprocated, "Yes, Kevin, I remember, how are you doing?" Jed York was there, as gracious and charming as ever.

"Do you mind if I get a picture with you both?" Roger and Jed posed with me for a photo, a lasting remembrance of this culminating moment.

The Ribbon-Cutting ceremony was to begin shortly. I walked over with former Mayor Patty Mahan's 80-year old mother and her grandson. We briefly got lost in the crowd before being escorted in the right direction. We took our assigned seats. There were several familiar faces, many having volunteered in various leading ways on the Measure J campaign. I was disappointed that all those devotees who toiled so fervently for this cause could not be here as well, so they, too, could stand alongside former mayors, managers, council members and other community leaders.

Seated on the field, the sun shined bright, it was quite a warm day. But in the midst of this shiney new edifice on a glorious day, joy exceeded the heat. Kicking off the ceremony proper, 49ers CEO & President Jed York

CharlesV Bergh,
CEO, Levis Strauss

With Larry MacNeil, Lisa Gillmor, and Lisa Lang

With Del Fontana, Peggy Parkin, Dorothy Rosa

Michael Short/San Francisco Chronicle/Polaris

kindly acknowledged me: "I appreciate the fact that Kevin Moore was the first person that really reached out to the Niners and said you have to look at Santa Clara for a football stadium."

The red ribbon was cut with gold scissors, with each red streamer fluttering gently in the hot breeze. Colorful confetti once again rained down as it had at the Groundbreaking. Music played loudly though I can't remember exactly what song (somewhere in the set was Coldplay's *Viva la Vida),* and the songs moved the clapping congregation, encouraging thrones to sway with the music. The stadium was officially opened. I almost expected to see the 49ers come charging out onto the field.

After the formal ribbon-cutting we were on our way out when a cameraman from Channel 7, a Santa Clara resident himself, came up, gave me a man-hug and complimented me. "Great job, Kev, must feel good about what you see here."

Then, out of nowhere, Channel 5's Len Ramirez stepped into my path, "Kevin, I'd like to interview you."

"Sure Len, I'll be happy to give you an interview, but only if Lisa Gillmor can join us too. He paused, "All right, if that's what you prefer."

"Yes, Len, it's important to have Lisa with me on the interview."

Lisa was chatting a short distance away and as I moved toward her Rob Fladeboe with Channel 4 approached me, "Kevin, good to see you, how about an interview?"

"Yeah, sure, but let me bring in Lisa Gillmor."

"Sure, Lisa's great."

I took Lisa by her arm, "Lisa, I have us an interview."

"No, Kev, you do it."

Steering Lisa with both a smile and gentle push on the back, I guided her toward Rob and Len who'd both waited very patiently. "We're doing this interview together."

We gave credit to the residents of Santa Clara and those City leaders who had built the infrastructure and paved the way before us. We felt proud we could publicly express the gratitude they deserved for their contributions. We were happy that the construction workers on the Stadium were also acknowledged with a grand applause from the attendees. The Stadium's two-year construction was a feat in itself. I was pleased to be at this event side-by-side with my friend, Lisa, who was instrumental in this major feat.

We then sought out folks whom we wanted to see, and avoided a few others. The ongoing ceremony offered opportunities for photo ops, and there was a food buffet and other activities. Dispensing with these further festivites, Lisa and I hightailed it out of Levi's Stadium. We were looking forward to the Black Tie Gala coming in two days.

The 49ers gave my father this brick with a note that read "Jack, First brick... is yours."

"A job worth doing is worth doing well."
– Jack Moore, Dad

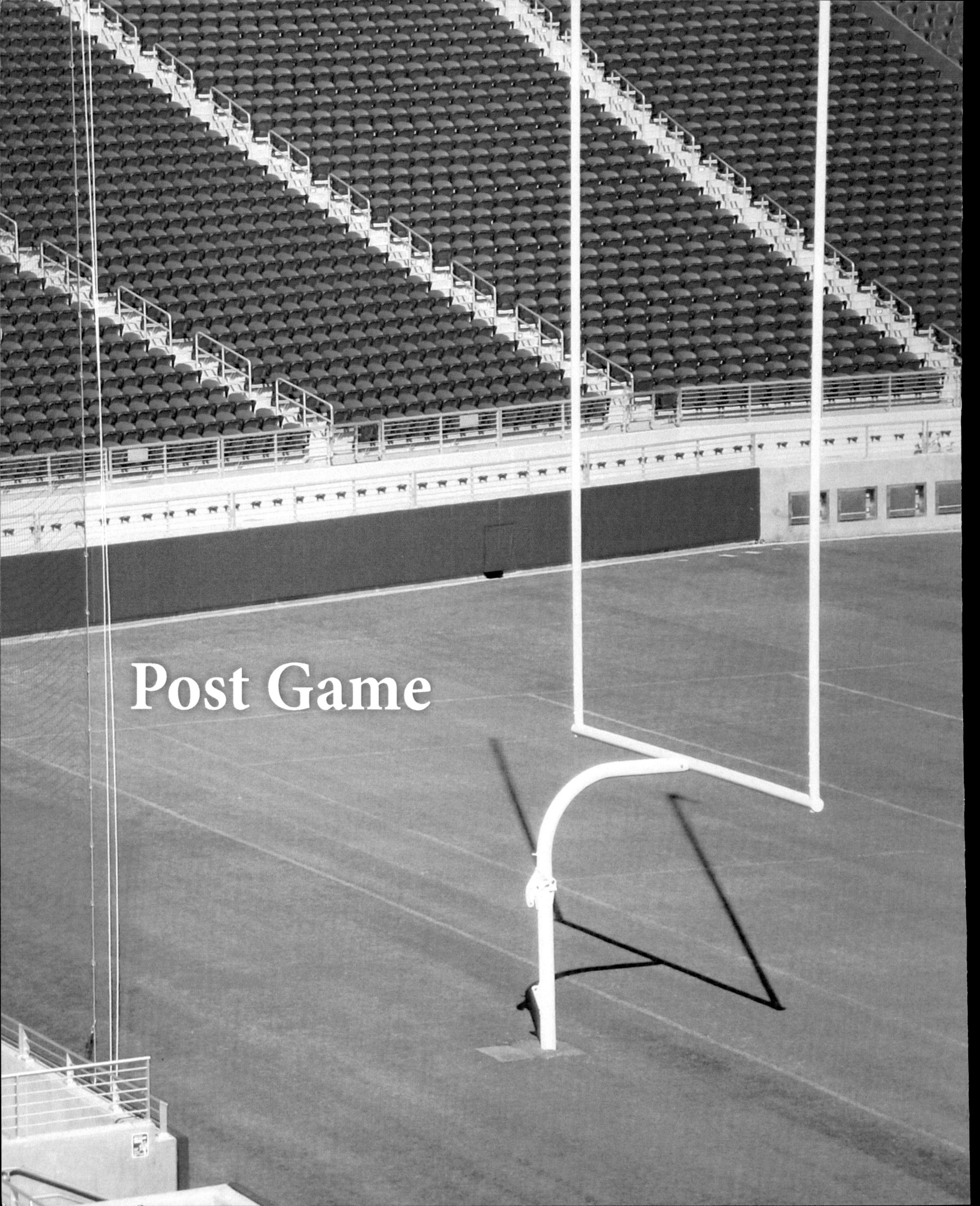

Post Game

IN THE END ZONE WITH THE 49ERS

Two days later, July 19, 2014, was the exclusive Black Tie Gala formally celebrating the completion and naming of Levi's Stadium. That morning my wife, Julee, who had selected one beautiful dress, decided to switch to another dress. The new gown was stunning but needed to be slightly tailored and pressed. I tried to be patient and assist. That evening Julee looked absolutely gorgeous, the most beautiful woman in the world. I dressed in my tux, relieved that it still fit. We hired a dog-sitter since we expected to be out late; Trudy would not be attending tonight! We were an elegant couple ready to put on the Ritz as we headed to Levi's Stadium in the BMW (yes, that same infamous driving machine).

Motorized SF cable cars met us in Lot A to transport attendees to the entrance where a red carpet had been rolled out, lending an Oscars-like air of glamour and excitement. Cameras were flashing. We wondered if the Gala was choreographed by some Hollywood producer.

Women in their stiletto heels all seem challenged to walk, and so us men had to adjust to parading slowly down the red carpet. I became conscious of being on a date with my wife, the best date of my life. I truly had a mindset to make this night special for Julee. We found a cozy corner in the crowded clubroom to sip drinks and nibble on hors d'oeuvres. We were joined by Lisa Gillmor and my sister Emmy, who was exceptionally effervescent and she must have taken a thousand pictures. Jed York came by and invited me for lunch the following week. He insisted we attend the opening of the SF 49ers Museum. He was rightly proud of all the Stadium offered.

I'm not a person to follow celebrities, so Julee and I made a point to hang back. We kept running into the President & CEO of Levi Strauss & Co., Chip Bergh. His named recalled the "Chip" of *My Three Sons* but the comparison stopped there. Chip had on a black Levi's jacket that looked really cool on him; at the Ribbon Cutting he wore a gold jacket that was cool, too.

The crowd was large though it was an exclusive event. There was an endless assortment of food and beverages. I had a beer, my wife had champagne. My friend Myron Von Raesfeld joined us, but his wife was unable to attend so we made plans for this big guy named Pete to *sneak in* as Pam. The night before when we learned Pam wasn't attending, we had Pete text Myron, "Hey Myron, can I be your girl for the night?" These were the friends

Jerry Smith Santa Clara University Women's Head Soccer Coach with his wife Brandi Chastain, Olympic & World Cup Champion; Heidi & Jay Leupp

My wife Julee and I

John Legend

Coach Tomsula and wife Julie

Y.A. Tittle and Daughter Diane

Coach Harbaugh and wife Sarah

Photos courtesy of the 49ers

with whom we dined, drank, and partied. I ran into my good buddy Ronnie Lott and his gorgeous wife and we had a nice chat, and took pictures with our significant others. In the soon-to-be Niners locker room was a concentration of high profile politicians and celebrities posing for photographs. Back at party central, a band played on and John Legend took the stage and sang his greatest hits.

We ascended to the second floor of the Tower Suites to better view the pyrotechnics. As the fireworks started exploding, I thought back to that moment eight years ago when a 49ers announcement lit a fuse and virtual fireworks crackled over the team's possible move to Santa Clara. Seeing the expanse of the Stadium in the glow of fireworks was magical. Folks all seemed to echo similar words: "Wow, this Stadium is incredible, more impressive than ever; it's palatial."

We quickly desired to boogie down to the dance floor strategically laid upon the playing field. One could actually exit *The BNY Club* right onto the field, that is, if one could resist stopping at the artistically lighted bar, while passing the elegant food and dessert. A disc jockey was playing records on the dance floor, classic songs, all driving the beat to dance. People were smiling, bumping, slapping high-fives, even the most serious of City employees were letting loose. The scene was one of thrill, wonder, utter amazement.

After dancing and drinks, a moment afforded me opportunity to shuffle off in a direction presumed to be off-limits, but no one stopped me. I strolled into the end zone by myself. Standing in the end zone, looking up at the goal post, the Stadium surrounding me on all sides, I thought out loud, "Thank you, God. We did it; Santa Clara built a stadium, this incredible Stadium, a home to the San Francisco 49ers. Thank you, God, thank you." Then I prayed in gratitude and in blessing a "Hail Mary." Looking into the night sky with music softly in the distance, I heard play in my own head *A Nightingale Sang in Berkeley Square.* That evening, a nightnigale surely sang in Santa Clara. My

My beautiful wife Julee

heart rode up-and-down like a merry-go-round. Emotions overpowered me, I was humbled by the All.

Reflecting for a moment more, I looked at this accomplishment in amazement. How much had come together that had no business coming together. There was a sense of synchronicity, of people and forces having converged into this new reality. I wondered, "Was this fate? Was an invisible hand at work? The reality was more spectacular than the dream itself, and the journey to this time and place was profound."

I slowly walked back to the Stadium Club and found my wife. Julee asked, "Where have you been?"

"I was in the end zone with Dwight Clark, watching as he caught a Hail Mary pass from Joe Montana." Julee looked at me a little perplexed. I winked and smiled, "Time to go home, dear."

Frederic Larson/San Francisco Chronicle/Polaris

AFTERWORD

In this new millennium, when we think of California cities, San Diego, San Jose, Santa Clara, San Francisco–we often forget their origination as the Mission Trail established by Franciscan priests and brothers. We may have never heard the story of the saints for whom these cities were named. Two of those saints, Francis and Clare, were spiritual brother and sister who shared a dream and lived a journey. Through a vision, Francis restored brick by brick the little Church of San Damiano which he then gave to Clare as a home for her order of religious. Clare in turn hosted Francis often, providing him hospice. How fitting these namesakes, Santa Clara and San Francisco, should be so united in the 21st century.

"Start by doing what's necessary; then do what's possible; and suddenly you are doing the impossible." – St. Francis of Assisi

ACKNOWLEDGEMENTS

This book was more than a moment in time, more than a campaign for a professional sports team to come to Santa Clara. This book is in part "My Life." Please indulge this author with the privilege of recognizing the many good people who have blessed my life, contributing directly or indirectly to this story. I give credit first to God, the Lord Jesus Christ and Mother Mary for many blessings, embracing these below:

My beautiful and intelligent, true companion, wife Julee; our precious four-legged "daughter" Trudy, Mom and Dad, the Moore Clan and extended family, with sister Emmy and niece Gina kindly contributing to this book.

The residents of the City of Santa Clara, The Mission City! All the Community Leaders who provided leadership, many having laid the foundation for Levi's Stadium.

All current and former Santa Clara Mayors, Council Members and City Staff, particularly Lisa and Gary Gillmor, Larry and Jerry Marsalli, Patty and John Mahan, Eddie Sousa, Jamie Matthews, Pat Kolstad, Gary Hansen, Dom Caserta, Joe Kornder, Debi Davis, Teresa O'Neill, Don Von Raesfeld, Jennifer Sparacino, Julio Fuentes, Ren Nosky, Chief Mike Sellers.

State Senator Elaine Alquist, Larry Stone, Dr. Elliot Lepler, Steve Van Dorn, Miles Barber, Manny Ferguson, Steve Lodge, Terry Carmody, Ray Collishaw, Don Callejon, Larry Wolfe; Rod Diridon, Sr. and Jr.; Neil Struthers, Jerry Smith, Brandi Chastain, Cindy Schelcher.

The San Francisco 49ers organization, family and Faithful, for believing in me and the people of Santa Clara, that we would provide the best location for a new home. The York and DeBartolo families, Ronnie Lott, Dwight Clark, Brent Jones, Kenna Turner, John Faylor, Y.A. Tittle, Lisa Lang, Gideon Yu, Fred Formosa, Larry McNeil, Andy Dolich, Ted Robinson, Patty English.

The Measure J campaign Team, particularly Ed McGovern, Rich Robinson, Myron Von Raesfeld and the AWESOME volunteers.

To all my friends, especially Team Fun: the Millers, Sasos, Fines, Blairs, McCarthys, Georges, Mezzettis, Enfantinos, Kellys, Olsons, Caloiaros, Lemucchis, Burts; along with Dane, Stace, Sand, Amy, Beaser, Jen, Dayna, Christina; also Tom-Ass, Guy Bone, KP, JR, Tanya, Rena, Soseek, Jory, Sandy; The Poker Group; Maki and Roshun Fuzel; JP who took me to my first Giants game at the Stick and Richard Caswell and David LeBaron for taking me to many games.

My teachers, professors and administrators, many from St. Justin, Archbishop Mitty High School, Chaminade and Santa Clara Universities; notably George Santich, Fr. Jack Russi S.M., Brother Elmer Dunsky S.M., Gary Cramton, Steve Davis, Ruth Davis, Joan Flynn, Vinnette Ai, Dr. Unni, Dr. Robert Smith, Mrs. Mack, Gary Braia, Judy Semas, Ms. Kennedy, Dr. Robert Brancatelli, Bill Sullivan, Steve Hyndman, Chris and Kathy.

The Media, notably Robert Handa, John Coté, Mark Purdy, Rob Fadeboe, Lloyd LaCuesta, Len Ramirez, Julie Patel, Carolyn Schuck, Henry Tennenbaum, Raj Mathai, Marianne Favro and Karina Rusk.

Michael Fallon, teacher, coach, rock promoter, friend, writer – who helped drive the writing and publishing of this book; W.J. "Bill" Parolini, writer, director, advisor; Nick Martinez and Rimo Moreno; Jo Ann Wall, JSTS Transcription; Jim Otis and Mark Gardner, Iguana; Ray R. Rodriquez, Jr.; Jeff Paul, Paul McNamara, Melvin Macias, Chuck Hattemer; Br. Thomas C. Bracco S.J., Susan Fornoff, David Gillmor, John Dixon, Ed Strine.

Again, thank you to all and to those others who touched my life but could not be listed here.

REFERENCES

Bodo, Murray. Francis ~ the Journey and the Dream. Cincinnati: St. Anthony Messenger Press, 1972

City of Santa Clara: http://santaclaraca.gov/

City of Santa Clara: Levi's Stadium: http://santaclaraca.gov/index.aspx?page=1197

Santa Clara Proud, a supplement of Santa Clara Weekly, May 2014

Six *San Jose Mercury News* headlines & photos: Used with permission of the *San Jose Mercury News,* Copyright © 2014. All rights reserved.

Three *San Francisco Chronicle* / Polaris photos, by Fredric Larson, by Michael Macor, by Michael Short: Used with permission of the *San Francisco Chronicle,* Copyright © 2014. All rights reserved.

Image from the 49ers Museum photographed with permission by Michael Fallon; Levi's Stadium photographs by Michael Fallon

Visit Levi's® Stadium Tours and 49ers Museum Presented by Sony: LEVISSTADIUM.COM

City of Santa Clara images photographed by W.J. Parolini

Gala Photo by Emmy Moore Minister

All episodes derived from the knowledge of the author, writers, friends and associates; and from memorabilia the author collected over the past 25 years. Some general supplemental information gleaned from articles *in Santa Clara Weekly, San Jose Mercury News, San Francisco Chronicle, Wikipedia.*

ABOUT THE AUTHOR AND WRITERS
~ A Story Unto Itself

What "moore" can be said about Kevin Moore than you have already gleaned from your reading? First and foremost, he is an amazing storyteller, almost in the Irish-tradition of a shenachie. Kev is a life-long resident of Santa Clara. He attended St. Justin School, then Archbishop Mitty High School. At Chaminade University Kevin was a three sport-college athlete and Student Body President. He later received an M.A. from Santa Clara University. Kev is a life-long baseball, basketball and football fan; a devoted follower of the San Francisco Giants, Oakland A's and Forty Niners, obviously. He married Julee, similarly his equal as a true Giants fan. Kevin first became politically involved with Santa Clara Parks & Recreation Commission, then became a Councilman and Vice-Mayor. He was co-founder of the Santa Clara Youth Soccer Park and the San Tomas Aquino-Saratoga Creek Trail. Earlier stadium attempts with the Giants and the A's honed his knowledge and skills an dealing with professional sports franchises. Kevin made the first overture to the San Francisco 49ers and was a driving force throughout the venture. Having termed out as council member, Kevin remains an advocate for fair politics and is actively involved in several professional pursuits including business consulting, real estate and land use, writing books and screen plays. Nonetheless, he almost never passes up an opportunity to attend a sporting event.

Kevin has received the Santa Clara Chamber of Commerce Distinguished Community Leadership Award, the International Swim Hall of Fame Service Award, and was appointed to the Super Bowl 50 Host Committee.

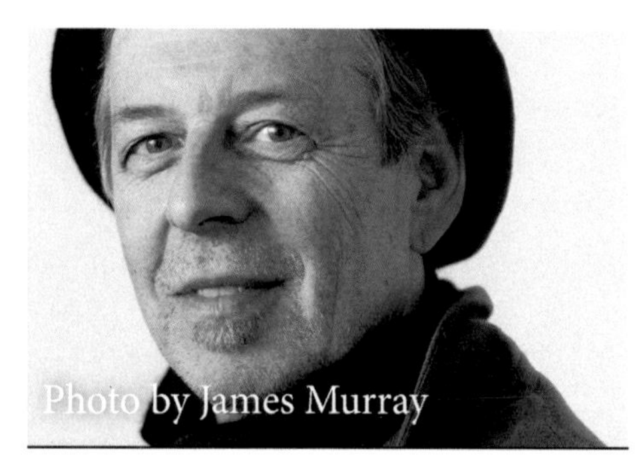

Michael Fallon first taught and coached at St. Lawrence Academy in Santa Clara, where his sports teams played against Kevin Moore's teams at St. Justins. Michael moved to Mitty HS in 1981 as Student Activities Director and Religious Studies teacher where he taught and coached Kevin in his senior year. Michael maintained a mentorship role with Kevin during Moore's "formative years" at Chaminade and Santa Clara University. Their association deepened into friendship in ensuing years, with periodic trips to Candlestick Park. Michael left AMHS in 1990, coincidentally, the year Kevin arrived. In 1997 Michael wrote and published *The Definitive St. Patrick's Day Festivity Book.* Kevin, being of Irish stock himself, became the book's biggest promoter, accompanying Michael to Irish book fairs up and down the state. Also in 1997, Michael began teaching Sociology at Mission College in Santa Clara California, and in 2002 commenced his current tenure at San Jose State University where he is now Director of Community Learning & Leadership. Michael met Bill Parolini as both walked their dogs in Carmichael Park. Michael lives with his wife (and dogs) in Santa Clara.

W. J. Parolini is an award-winning writer and filmmaker. He assisted Michael and Kevin as they penned this book, contributed photographs to this project and initiated the InDesign work. Bill now lives in North Carolina.

Mark Gardner, Iguana Design and Print, is a highly skilled Graphic Designer whose extensive work and contributions to the book design, construction, and printing were indispensable.